AMERICAN POLITICAL, ECONOMIC, AND SECURITY ISSUES

VOTING AND ELECTION REFORM

AMERICAN POLITICAL, ECONOMIC, AND SECURITY ISSUES

Additional books in this series can be found on Nova's website under the Series tab.

Additional E-books in this series can be found on Nova's website under the E-books tab.

AMERICAN POLITICAL, ECONOMIC, AND SECURITY ISSUES

VOTING AND ELECTION REFORM

NICOLE P. FLETCHER
EDITOR

Nova Science Publishers, Inc.
New York

For permission to use material from this book please contact us:
Telephone 631-231-7269; Fax 631-231-8175
Web Site: http://www.novapublishers.com

Library of Congress Cataloging-in-Publication Data

Voting and election reform / editor, Nicole P. Fletcher.
p. cm.
Includes index.
ISBN 978-1-61324-640-5 (hardcover)
1. Voting--United States. 2. Elections--United States. 3. Election law--United States. I. Fletcher, Nicole P.
JK1976.V66 2011
324.6'50973--dc22

2011015646

Published by Nova Science Publishers, Inc. † New York

CONTENTS

PREFACE

This book focuses on voting practices, election reform and local election officials who are critical to the administration of federal elections and the implementation of the Help America Vote Act of 2002 (HAVA). Topics discussed include how local election officials view election reform; the Help America Vote Act of 2002 and elections reform issues; the history and implementation of the National Voter Registration Act of 1993; and the constitutional authority and limitations relevant to Congress standardizing the administration of voter registration, balloting, tabulating and reporting election results.

Chapter 1- Local election officials (LEOs) are critical to the administration of federal elections and the implementation of the Help America Vote Act of 2002 (HAVA, P.L. 107-252). Three surveys of LEOs were performed by academic institutions in collaboration with the Congressional Research Service. Although care needs to be taken in interpreting the results, they may have implications for several policy issues, such as how election officials are chosen and trained, the best ways to ensure that voting systems and election procedures are sufficiently effective, secure, and voter-friendly, and whether adjustments should be made to HAVA requirements. Major results include the following:

Chapter 2- Since the November 2000 presidential election, previously obscure details of voting and vote counting have been the focus of ongoing public attention and legislative action at the state and federal levels. The Help America Vote Act (HAVA, P.L. 107-252) was enacted in October 2002, and the states have made additional changes to election laws and procedures since then. Numerous bills to amend HAVA have been considered in the Congress as well, although only one has been enacted that made a minor change to the law. HAVA created a new federal agency (the Election Assistance Commission), set requirements for various aspects of election administration, and provided federal funding. However, the law did not supplant state and local control over election administration.

Chapter 3- After the passage of the Voting Rights Act of 1965 (42 U.S.C. § 1973–1973aa-6, see http://www.law.cornell.edu/uscode/html/ uscode 42/usc_sup 01 42 10 20 20 I-A.html), legislation had been urged for over two decades that would create a national voter registration system designed to make registration easier and more uniform from state to state. The National Voter Registration Act of 1993 (NVRA, P.L. 103-31, 107 Stat.77, [42 U.S.C. § 1973gg et seq., see http://www.law.cornell.edu/uscode/ html/ uscode42/usc_sup 01 42 10 20 20 I-H.html]), the so-called "motor-voter" bill, was signed into law by President Clinton on May 20, 1993. It required states to establish voter registration procedures for federal elections so that eligible citizens might apply to register to vote (1) simultaneously while applying for a driver's license, (2) by mail, and (3) at selected state and local offices that serve the public. The law took effect on January 1, 1995, for most states.

Chapter 4- Events surrounding the 2000 presidential election have led to increased scrutiny of voting procedures in the United States, including efforts to establish national standards for issues such as the administration of voter registration, balloting, tabulating, and reporting election results. This report focuses on the constitutional authority and limitations relevant to Congress standardizing these and other election procedures.

In: Voting and Election Reform
Editor: Nicole P. Fletcher

ISBN: 978-1-61324-640-5

Chapter 1

HOW LOCAL ELECTION OFFICIALS VIEW ELECTION REFORM: RESULTS OF THREE NATIONAL SURVEYS*

Eric A. Fischer and Kevin J. Coleman

SUMMARY

Local election officials (LEOs) are critical to the administration of federal elections and the implementation of the Help America Vote Act of 2002 (HAVA, P.L. 107-252). Three surveys of LEOs were performed by academic institutions in collaboration with the Congressional Research Service. Although care needs to be taken in interpreting the results, they may have implications for several policy issues, such as how election officials are chosen and trained, the best ways to ensure that voting systems and election procedures are sufficiently effective, secure, and voter-friendly, and whether adjustments should be made to HAVA requirements. Major results include the following:

The demographic characteristics of LEOs differ from those of other government officials. Almost three-quarters are women, and 5% are minorities. Most do not have a college degree, and most were elected, although those characteristics appear to be changing. Some results

---

* This is an edited, reformatted and augmented version of a Congressional Research Services publication, CRS Report for Congress R41667, from www.crs.gov, dated March 4, 2011.

suggest areas of potential improvement such as in training and participation in professional associations.

LEOs believed that the federal government has too great an influence on the acquisition of voting systems, and that local elected officials have too little. Their concerns increased from 2004 to 2006 about the influence of the media, political parties, advocacy groups, and vendors. Concern about the influence of these groups increased again, slightly, from 2006 to 2008.

LEOs were highly satisfied with whatever voting system they used but were less supportive of other kinds. Their satisfaction declined from 2004 to 2006 for all systems except lever machines, but rebounded in 2008. They also rated their primary voting systems as very accurate, secure, reliable, and voter- and pollworker-friendly, no matter what system they used. However, the most common incident reported by respondents in both the 2006 and 2008 elections was malfunction of a direct recording (DRE) or optical scan (OS) electronic voting system. The incidence of long lines at polling places was highest in jurisdictions using DREs. Most DRE users did not believe that voter-verified paper audit trails (VVPAT) should be required, but nonusers believed they should be. However, the percentage of DRE users who supported VVPAT increased from 2004 to 2008, and more VVPAT users were satisfied with them in 2008 than in 2006.

On average, LEOs mildly supported requiring photo identification for all voters and believed it would make elections more secure, even though they strongly believed that it will negatively affect turnout and did not believe that voter fraud is a problem in their jurisdictions.

In all three surveys, LEOs believed that HAVA is making moderate improvements in the electoral process. The level of support declined from 2004 to 2006 but increased to its highest point in 2008. LEOs reported that HAVA has increased the accessibility of voting but has made elections more complicated and has increased their cost, though fewer believed so in 2008 than in 2006. LEOs spent much more time preparing for the election in 2008 than in 2004. They also believed that the increased complexity of elections is hindering recruitment of pollworkers. Most found the activities of the Election Assistance Commission (EAC) that HAVA created moderately important, and that its helpfulness improved from 2006 to 2008. Their assessment of the statewide voter-registration database was neutral in 2006 but positive in 2008. They believed that it was more accurate and fair than their previous registration system.

INTRODUCTION

U.S. elections are highly decentralized, with much of the responsibility for election administration residing with local election officials (LEOs). There are thousands of such officials, many of whom are responsible for all aspects of election administration in their local jurisdictions—including voter registration, recruiting pollworkers, running each election, and choosing and purchasing new voting systems.

These officials are therefore critical not only to the successful administration of federal elections, but also to the implementation of the Help America Vote Act of 2002 (HAVA, P.L. 107-252), the Uniform and Overseas Citizens Absentee Voting Act (UOCAVA, P.L. 99-410, as amended) and other federal statutes. Nevertheless, there has been little objective information on the perceptions and attitudes of LEOs about election reform. Such information may be useful to Congress in deliberations about federal election reform activities.

This report discusses the results of three scientific opinion surveys that were designed to help fill that gap in knowledge about principal local election officials.[1] The surveys were performed pursuant to projects sponsored by the Congressional Research Service (CRS). The projects were developed in collaboration with and the surveys performed by faculty and students at the George Bush School of Government and Public Service at Texas A&M University, and the Center for Applied Social Research at the University of Oklahoma. The university teams developed and administered the surveys, in consultation with CRS, to samples of LEOs from all 50 states, with a response rate of approximately 40% for each survey. The responses were analyzed by CRS for purposes of this report. See the *Appendix* for information on the methods used in the surveys and analyses.

The surveys were administered following the 2004, 2006, and 2008 federal elections. While they were not identical, many of the questions were the same, and comparisons of the results are discussed where appropriate.[2] The findings may be useful to Congress as it considers funding for HAVA, oversight of its implementation, and possible revisions to current law.

The report begins with a description of some characteristics of local election officials and their jurisdictions. That is followed by a discussion of perceptions and attitudes of LEOs about the different kinds of voting systems used in different jurisdictions—lever machines, punchcard ballots, hand-counted paper ballots,[3] central-count optical scan (CCOS), precinct-count optical scan (PCOS), and direct-recording electronic (DRE) systems such as "touchscreens." The report then describes how HAVA has affected local jurisdictions and the opinions LEOs expressed about the law. The section after that discusses other election administration topics covered in the 2006 and 2008 surveys—preparations for election day, election-day incidents, characteristics of pollworkers, and attitudes about nonpartisan election administration. The final sections discuss caveats to consider in interpreting the results, and potential policy implications of the findings.

Characteristics of Local Election Officials and Their Jurisdictions

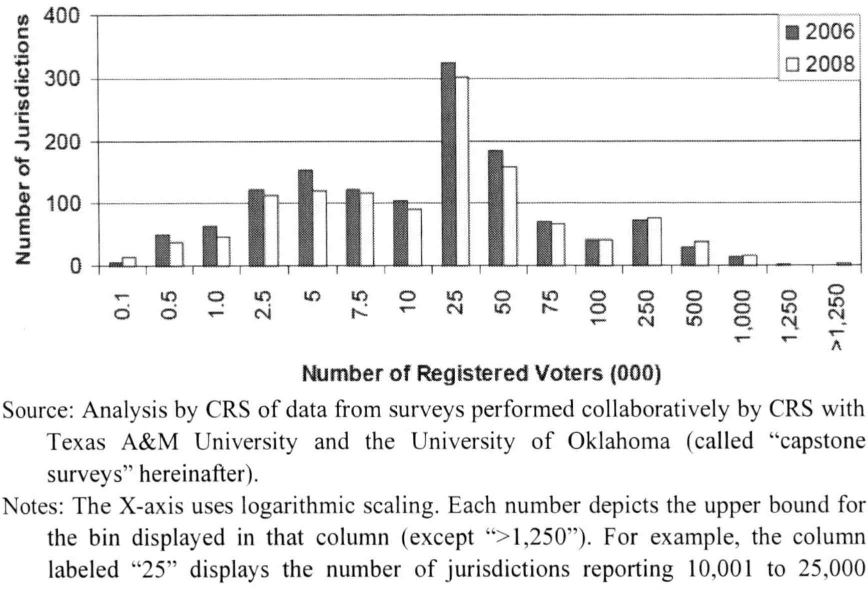

Source: Analysis by CRS of data from surveys performed collaboratively by CRS with Texas A&M University and the University of Oklahoma (called "capstone surveys" hereinafter).

Notes: The X-axis uses logarithmic scaling. Each number depicts the upper bound for the bin displayed in that column (except ">1,250"). For example, the column labeled "25" displays the number of jurisdictions reporting 10,001 to 25,000 registered voters. Throughout this report, bar or column graphs comparing results of the three surveys show data for 2004 in blue (color copies) or medium gray (black and white), for 2006 in burgundy or dark gray, and for 2008 in yellow or light gray.

Figure 1. Reported Number of Registered Voters per Jurisdiction.

There are about 9,000 local election jurisdictions in the United States.[4] In most states, they are counties or major cities, but in some New England and Upper Midwest states, they are small townships—for example, more than 1,800 townships in Wisconsin. The number of registered voters and polling places in a jurisdiction reported by LEOs also varies greatly (*Figure 1 and Figure 2*).

The reported number of registered voters ranged from fewer than 100 to more than 1 million, with a median of about 12,000 in 2006 and 13,000 in 2008.[5] That 8% increase was consistent with the reported 7%-10% increase in the number of registered voters nationwide during that period.[6]

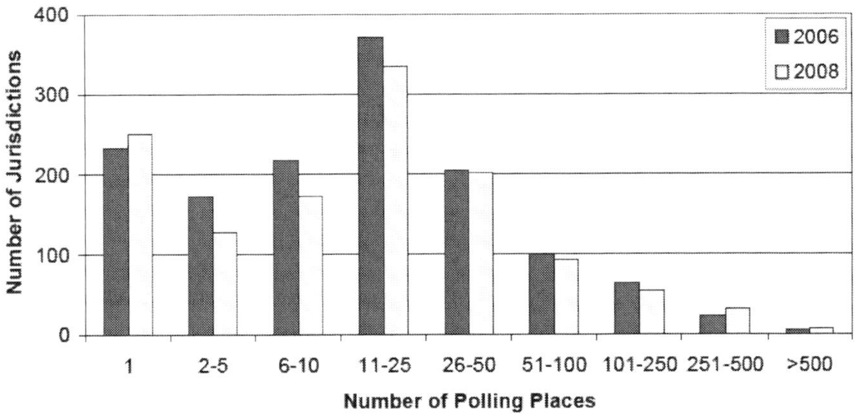

Source: Analysis by CRS of data from capstone surveys.

Figure 2. Reported Number of Polling Places per Jurisdiction, 2006 and 2008.

Although LEOs were not asked to report the number of voters in their jurisdictions in the 2004 survey, in 2008 they were asked how the number changed from 2004 to 2008. About two-thirds reported that the number of registered voters had increased between 2004 and 2008, and about one-fifth reported a decrease (*Figure 3*).

The number of polling places in a jurisdiction averaged about a dozen, ranging from 0 to 1,000 or more,[7] with about 15% of jurisdictions in each election having only one polling place and a similar percentage having more than 50. The number of election personnel working in a jurisdiction, in addition to the local election official, also varied greatly, from none to more than 10,000, including pollworkers. The 2008 survey also asked about the number of employees other than pollworkers. The median was 5, with a mean of 17 and a maximum of 800.

The number of registered voters, polling places, and pollworkers was about 10 times greater in county jurisdictions than in townships. LEOs from counties reported an average of about 56,000 registered voters, while those from townships averaged 6,000. There were 40 polling places per county on average, and 3 per township. Counties had about 290 pollworkers and townships 30.

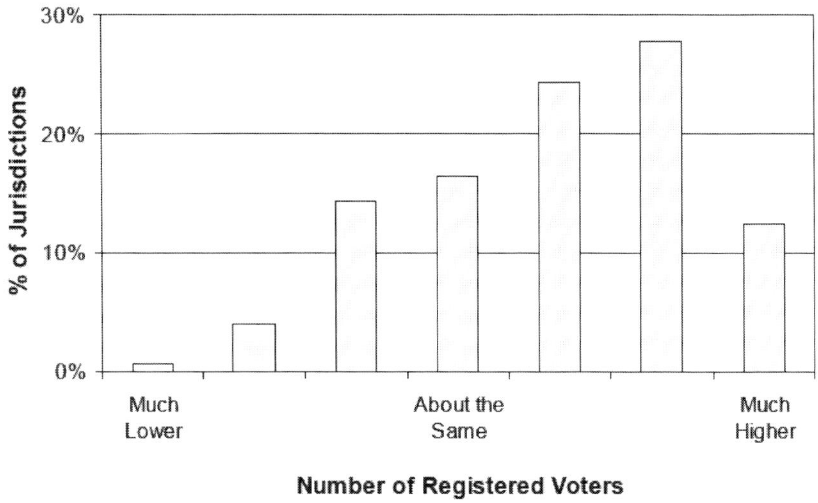

Source: Analysis by CRS of data from capstone surveys.

Figure 3. Change in the Number of Registered Voters from 2004 to 2008.

Given such diversity and other differences among states—such as wealth, population, and the role of state election officials—responsibilities and characteristics of LEOs are likely to vary greatly. Nevertheless, some patterns emerged from the surveys.

The Demographic Characteristics of Leos Differ from those of Other Government Officials

According to the survey results, the typical LEO is a white woman between 50 and 60 years old who is a high school graduate. She was elected to her current office, works full-time in election administration, has been in the profession for about 10 years, and earns under $60,000 per year. She belongs to a state-level professional organization but not a national one, and she believes that her training as an election official has been good to excellent.

As with any such description, the one above does not capture the diversity within the community surveyed: About one-quarter of LEOs are men, about

5% belong to minority groups, about 40% are college graduates, and about 10% have graduate degrees (see *Table 1*). LEOs range from under 25 to more than 80 years of age, and have served from 1 to 50 years. More than half were elected rather than appointed to their posts.[8] Reported salaries range from under $10,000 to more than $120,000. Most belong to at least one professional organization.

The demographic profile of LEOs is unusual, especially for a professional group. They differ from those of other local government employees. For example, according to U.S. Census figures, while women comprise a higher proportion of the local government workforce than men overall,[9] men comprise a higher proportion of local government general and administrative managers.[10] About 20% of those managers are members of minorities.[11] The patterns do not appear to be a result of the fact that most LEOs are elected, as the demographic characteristics of legislators appear to be largely similar to those for local government managers.[12]

Table 1. Comparison of Selected Demographic Characteristics of LEOs

Percentages of LEOs who…	2004	2006	2008
were elected.	65	58	53
worked full-time.	66	76	72
had served for more than 10 years in current position.	47	44	40
spent more than 20 hours per week on election duties.	41	47	49
did not belong to an association of election professionals.	30	26	31
were not college graduates.	60	59	56
possessed a graduate degree.	8.1	7.9	9.7
had a salary under $40,000.	47	39	37
were women.	75	77	76
were older than 50.	63	62	62
were not white.	5.6	5.4	6.5
professed a conservative political ideology.	51	47	44

Source: Analysis by CRS of data from capstone surveys.

Note: Bold type denotes statistically significant differences among the surveys.

The average tenure in the current position declined by about one year from 2004 to 2008, with the proportion of LEOs who had served for two years or less in their current positions rising to 18% in 2008 from 11% in 2004 (see *Figure 4*). Thus, there appeared to be a small increase in job turnover over the three elections.[13] However, there was no significant change in average age (*Figure 5*).

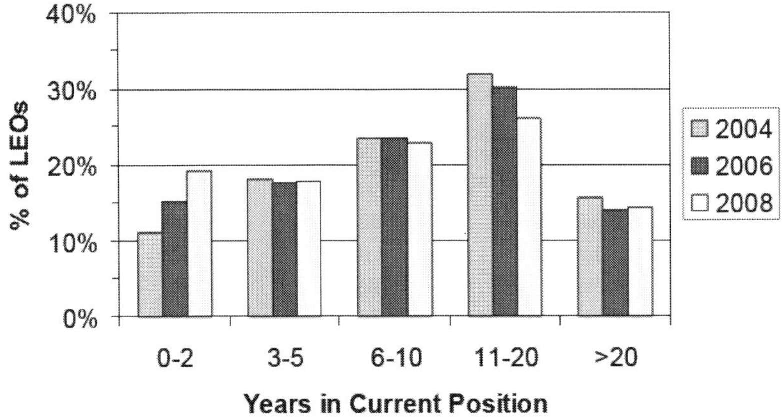

Source: Analysis by CRS of data from capstone surveys.

Figure 4. Length of Tenure of LEOs in Their Current Positions.

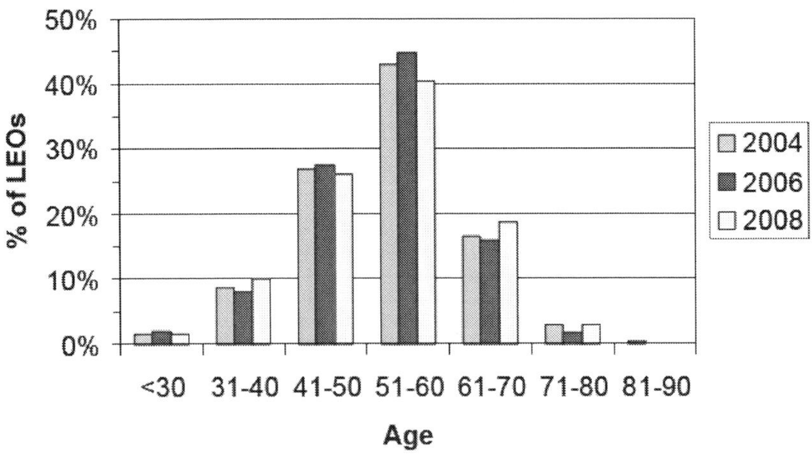

Source: Analysis by CRS of data from capstone surveys.

Figure 5. Age Distribution of LEOs.

Other trends across the surveys included a decrease in the proportion of LEOs who were elected, an increase in both the percentage who worked full time and in the amount of time they spent working on elections,[14] an increase in salary, and a decrease in the proportion who expressed a slightly to strongly conservative ideology.[15]

The survey was not designed to identify the causes of such changes, but at least some appear to be consistent with the impacts of federal and state election reform on local jurisdictions. That reform led to increased funding for election administration, changes in voting systems used by many jurisdictions, and an increased workload for many election officials. For example, the survey found that those who reported that they worked full-time on election administration increased from 66% in 2004 to 72% in 2008, while those who reported that they spent more than twenty hours per week on election duties increased from 41% to 49%.

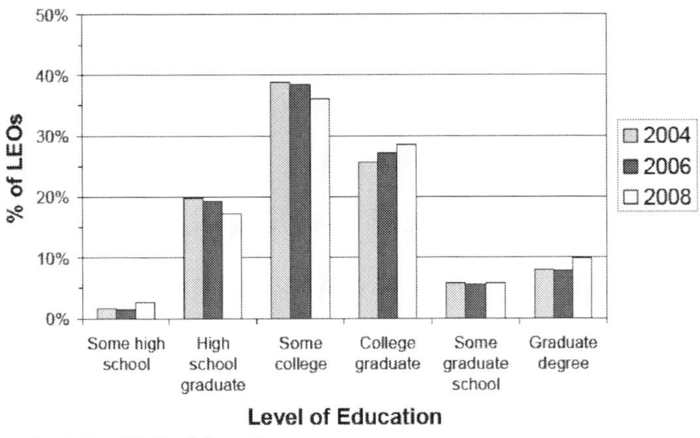

Source: Analysis by CRS of data from capstone surveys.

Figure 6. Level of Education Reported by LEOs.

The increasing complexity of elections and the increased federal role after the passage of HAVA have focused more attention on the role of professionalism in election administration. Given that change, it might be expected that election officials who began serving more recently would have more formal education than those who have served for longer periods. Such a pattern could yield a statistical association between the highest education level attained and the number of years in service as an election official. In fact, there was a small but significant relationship, with LEOs who did not have a college degree averaging 11-12 years of service and those with graduate degrees averaging 8-9 years. However, there was no significant change in the overall distribution of maximum education level over the three surveys (*Figure 6*).

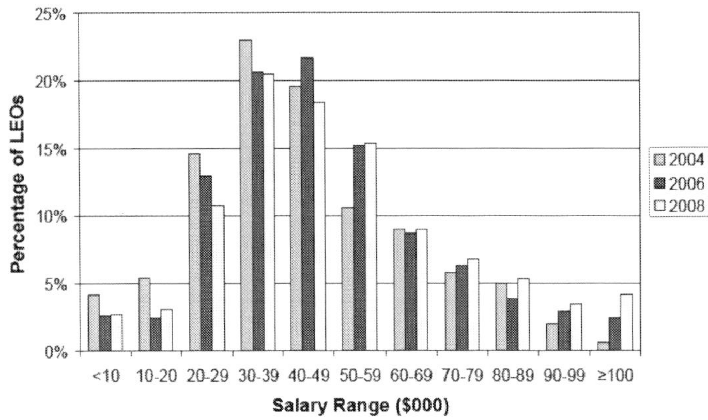

Source: Analysis by CRS of data from capstone surveys.

Figure 7. Salaries Reported by Local Election Officials.

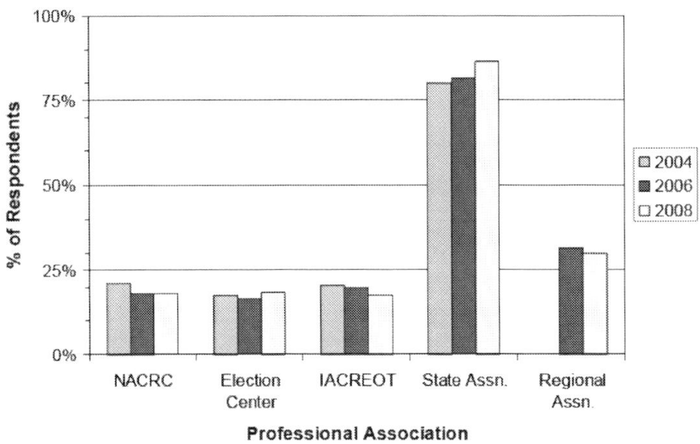

Source: Analysis by CRS of data from capstone surveys.

Note: Abbreviated names of associations are as follows: NACRC = National Association of County Recorders, Election Officials and Clerks; IACREOT = International Association of Clerks, Recorders, Election Officials and Treasurers. The choice of regional association was new for the 2006 survey. The data used in this graph include only those LEOs who indicated that they belonged to at least one professional association. See text.

Figure 8. Distribution of Memberships among LEOs Who Belong to One or More Professional Associations.

Reported salaries of LEOs increased about 7% per year, from an estimated average of $45,000 in 2004 to $51,000 in 2008 (*Figure 7*). LEOs in jurisdictions with larger numbers of voters tended to have somewhat higher salaries and education levels, and were more likely to be male. In 2008, the median salary for LEOs in jurisdictions below the median size in numbers of voters was $40- 50,000; it was $50,000-$60,000 for LEOs in larger jurisdictions. More than 20% of LEOs in larger jurisdictions had attended graduate school, while 10% of those from smaller jurisdictions had. LEOs were male in about 20% of jurisdictions below the median size, and in 30% of those above.

Fewer than Half of Leos Belonged to a National or International Association, but Most Belonged to a State Association

The survey also examined other factors related to election administration as a profession. More than two-thirds (70%-74%) of LEOs reported belonging to at least one professional association.[16] Of those, more than three-fourths belonged to a state association, 30% to a regional one, and about 20% to the three major national or international associations (see *Figure 8*). Altogether, about 40% of LEOs who belonged to at least one association were members of a national or international one, with more than half belonging only to a state or regional association.

In 2006, the percentage of LEOs reporting that they had a written job description was 43% for those who had been elected and 70% for those who had been appointed. Most LEOs reported a broad range of election-administration responsibilities beyond solely running elections. Most are also responsible for budgeting, personnel, and purchasing, for example (*Table 2*).[17]

Most LEOs received some initial training specifically designed to prepare them for their duties, but for most that training was less than 20 hours, and only one-fifth of LEOs were required to pass an examination (*Table 3*). Most have also received additional training beyond that initially provided. More than two-thirds of LEOs assessed that their training was good to excellent and resulted in moderate to substantial improvement in their effectiveness and ability to solve problems. More than four-fifths believed that training and experience are equally important in ensuring a successful election.

Table 2. Selected Election Administration Responsibilities Reported by LEOs, 2006

Responsibility	% Reporting
Managing poll workers and other election administrators	90
Serving as a liaison between my jurisdiction and state and federal election officials	90
Overseeing an election recount when necessary	88
Authorizing and adhering to a budget	83
Hiring poll workers and other election administrators	83
Reporting inappropriate conduct by voters or politicians at polling place	82
Maintaining contact with vendors	80
Maintaining the voter registration database	80
Purchasing election equipment	78
Maintaining an electronic voting system	76
Purchasing an electronic voting system	63
Additional duties not listed	57

Source: Analysis by CRS of data from capstone surveys.

Note: LEOs were asked to check all applicable items in the list of responsibilities presented in the table. The data presented may be overestimates. They are percentages of the 1,406 LEOs who responded to the question; 7% of LEOs who responded to the survey did not answer this question. Using the total number of 1,506 survey respondents would reduce the percentages by 4-6 points but would probably constitute underestimates.

Table 3. Training Reported by LEOs, 2006 and 2008

	Kind of Training			
	Initial		Additional	
Percentage of LEOs who…	2006	2008	2006	2008
received any training.	78	65	82	92
received > 20 hours of training.	43	46	52	63
received certification from training.	45	n/a	36	43
received mandatory training.	54	54	35	50
were required to pass an exam.	19	16	n/a	n/a

Source: Analysis by CRS of data from capstone surveys.

Note: n/a = not applicable. The question was not asked.

This result, shown in *Figure 9*, might reflect the impact of HAVA requirements, most of which went into effect in 2006. For example, election officials might have felt less well prepared by their training to implement HAVA in 2006 than in 2004, but the survey did not address that possibility. Other possible factors include increasing public attention to problems in election administration, and recent controversies about the reliability and security of voting systems. Two-fifths of respondents to the 2006 survey, and a third of 2008 respondents, commented on what kinds of additional training would be useful. The most common suggestions were for more training in technical and legal aspects of elections, and more "hands-on" training.

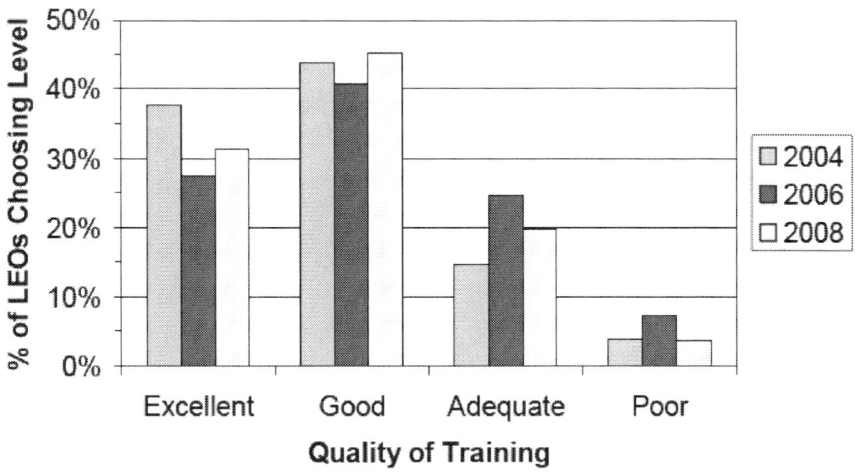

Source: Analysis by CRS of data from capstone surveys.

Figure 9. Assessments by LEOs of the Quality of the Training They Have Received.

Leos Were Less Satisfied with Their Training in 2006 and 2008 than in 2004

Given the increasing role of technology in elections, the surveys asked LEOs questions about their attitudes toward technology (*Figure 10*). Respondents believed that technology can be useful for government services, but were cautious about implementation.

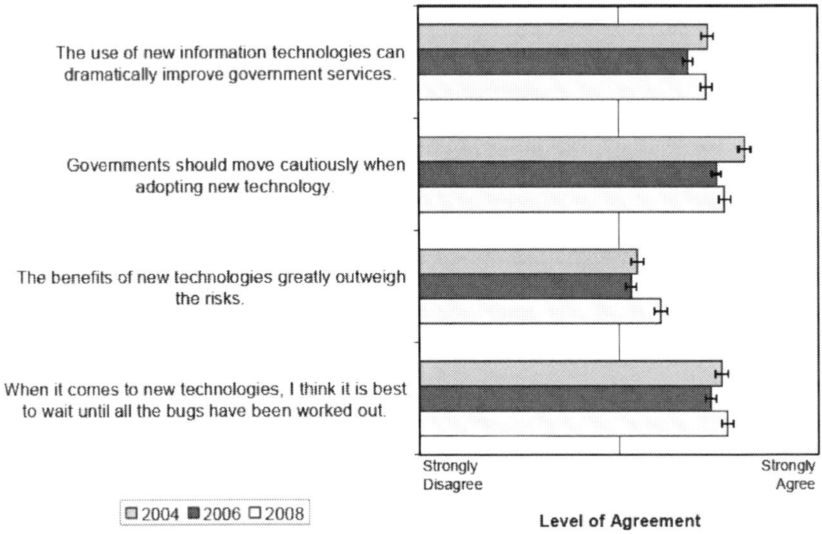

Source: Analysis by CRS of data from capstone surveys.

Note: Error bars on graphs in this report denote upper and lower 95% confidence limits for the average response (arithmetic mean).

Figure 10. Agreement/Disagreement of LEOs on Statements About Technology.

VOTING SYSTEMS

Current Voting System

The Use of Precinct-Count Optical Scan (PCOS) and Direct-Recording Electronic (DREs) Voting Systems Increased Substantially from 2004 To 2008

In 2004, more than half of jurisdictions used lever machines, punchcards, hand-counted paper ballots, or central-count optical scan (CCOS) as their primary voting systems. By 2008, that percentage had fallen by almost half, with lever machines decreasing by almost two-thirds,[18] paper ballots by half, CCOS by one-quarter,[19] and punchcards virtually disappearing by 2006 (see *Figure 11*). The proportion of jurisdictions using central-count optical scan (CCOS) decreased by almost half from 2004 to 2006, but that decline reversed in 2008.

Jurisdictions using PCOS and DREs increased substantially from 2004 to 2008, with a 50% increase for PCOS and more than two-thirds for DREs.[20] From 2006 to 2008, respondents reported a 5% increase in PCOS and a similar decrease in DREs, although those changes were not statistically significant.

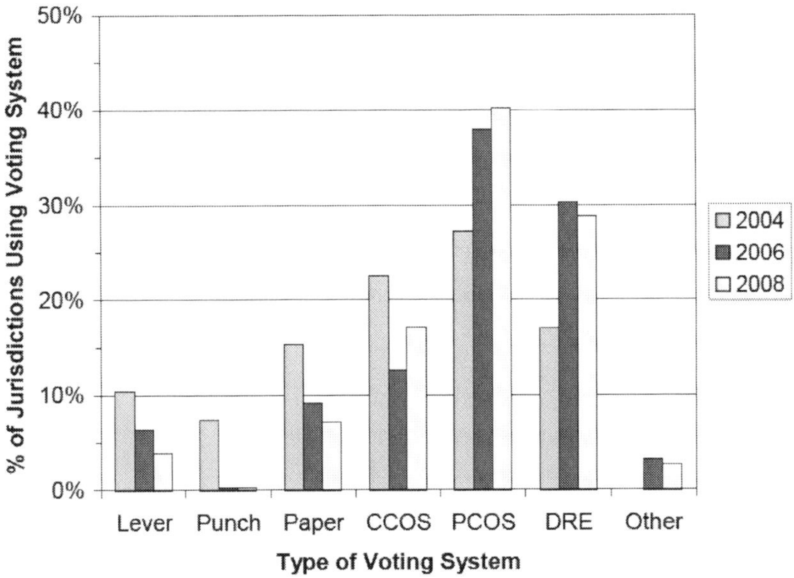

Source: Analysis by CRS of data from capstone surveys.

Note: Types of voting systems listed are as follows: Lever = mechanical lever machines; Punch = punchcard ballots; Paper = hand-counted paper ballots; CCOS = central-count optical scan systems; PCOS = precinct-count optical scan systems; DRE = direct-recording electronic systems; and Other = cases where the respondent checked "Other" and the primary voting system could not be determined from the written response—for example, the respondent wrote "DRE and OS." That might indicate, for example, that DREs were used only for accessibility, or that OS (optical scan) was used only for absentee ballots.

Figure 11. Percentages of Jurisdictions Using Different Kinds of Primary Voting Systems as Reported by LEOs.

The observed patterns are consistent with results from other sources.[21] The trends conform with expectations arising from HAVA requirements that emphasized improved usability, including prevention and correction of errors by voters in marking ballots, and accessibility of voting systems.[22] The increase in use of CCOS from 2006 and 2008 appears to run counter to that explanation, because unlike PCOS and DRE systems, CCOS does not provide assistance to voters in preventing errors. The cause of the increase is not clear, but two possible factors are the increase in "no-excuse" absentee voting (see the section on "Election Administration Issues") and the controversy about the security and reliability of DREs that have led many states to adopt paper-ballot requirements.[23]

Jurisdictions Appeared Reluctant to Change the Kinds of Voting Systems They Used

The average length of time jurisdictions have been using a particular kind of voting system varies greatly with the kind of system (Figure 12). The average length of use varies with the length of time a voting system has been available for use. At one extreme, jurisdictions with hand-counted paper ballots have used them for 80 to 100 years, on average. At the other, jurisdictions with DREs have had them under 10 years, on average.

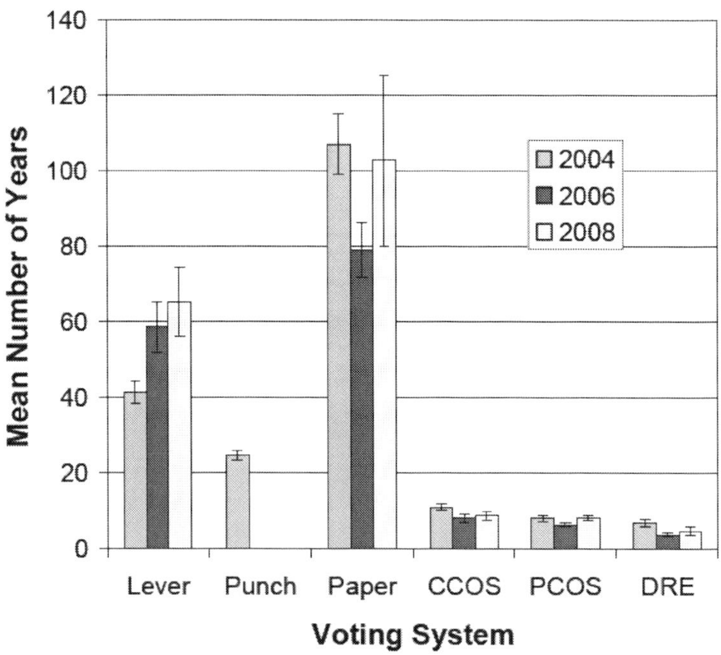

Source: Analysis by CRS of data from capstone surveys.

Note: See note for Figure 11 for an explanation of types of voting systems. Data on punchcard users is not presented for 2006 or 2008 because very few LEOs reported using them.

Figure 12. Average Length of Use of the Current Voting System as Reported by LEOs.

The pattern of use shown in Figure 12 suggests that jurisdictions do not readily change the kinds of voting systems they use. Before the 1990s, fewer than 10% of jurisdictions used optical scan and DRE voting systems.[24] On the one hand, such reluctance to change creates stability that may be beneficial to voters and administrators. On the other hand, it may mean that a particular kind of technology is used far longer than it should be, with increasing risks of negative consequences. For example, many of the problems associated with the 2000 presidential election were attributed to the continued use of outmoded or flawed technology, such as the punchcard systems in widespread use at the time.[25]

The causes of such long-term use patterns are complex and may include factors such as legal and budgetary constraints and various forms of transaction costs that would be incurred with any change. Such factors, if they continue to be important, may impede jurisdictions from taking advantage of the kinds of improvements that are likely to occur in voting technology over the next decade.

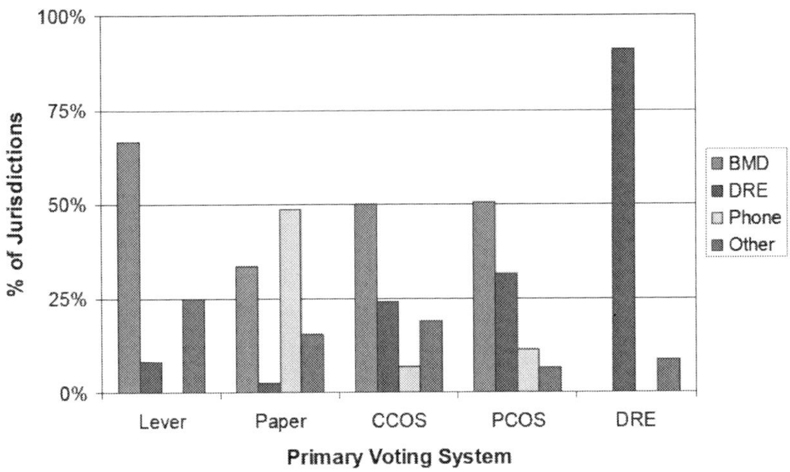

Source: Analysis by CRS of data from capstone surveys.

Notes: BMD = electronic ballot marking device; Phone = vote-by-phone system; Other = a system that could not be placed in one of the other categories based on the description provided in the survey response. See also note for Figure 11. Data on punchcard users is not presented because very few LEOs reported using them in 2008.

Figure 13. Kinds of Accessible Voting Systems Used by Jurisdictions with Different Primary Voting Systems, 2008.

The Kind of Accessible Voting System Used Varied with the Kind of Primary Voting System

In 2008, LEOs were asked about the voting systems they used to meet the HAVA accessibility requirement. The options presented were (1) an electronic ballot marking device (BMD), which uses a touchscreen or other computer interface to mark an optical-scan ballot; (2) a DRE; (3) a vote-by-phone voting system, in which the voter uses an automated telephone system to fill out the ballot; and (4) some other system, which the LEO was asked to describe.[26] As *Figure 13* shows, the kinds of accessible voting systems used varied depending on the kind of primary voting system used in the jurisdiction.[27] About 40% of responding jurisdictions reported using DREs as their accessible systems. Not surprisingly, most of those also used them as their primary systems.

A slightly lower percentage of respondents, 37%, reported using BMDs for accessibility, and it was most commonly used in lever-machine jurisdictions. While most optical-scan jurisdictions might be expected to use BMDs, only about half reported doing so. About 12% of jurisdictions used vote-by-phone, with the majority of those having hand-counted paper ballots as their primary system.

Table 4. Relative Use of Accessible Rather than Other Voting Machines by Voters without Disabilities, 2008

Accessible Voting System	Percentage of Jurisdictions		
	Less	The Same	More
DRE	52%	31%	18%
Phone	72%	17%	10%
BMD	76%	19%	5%
Other	61%	32%	7%
Total	64%	25%	11%

Source: Analysis by CRS of data from capstone surveys.

Notes: LEOs were asked the extent to which accessible voting systems were used by voters without disabilities, on a scale of -5 (much less) to +5 (much more), with 0 meaning "about the same." Data presented are sums of frequencies as follows: Less = -5 to -1, The Same = 0, and More = 1 to 5. See also note for Figure 13.

Three-quarters of jurisdictions reported having one accessible machine per polling place. About one-fifth used two, and about one in twenty used three. Most LEOs reported that voters without disabilities used accessible machines less than other machines, and about 40% reported that they used them much less. In jurisdictions using DREs as the accessible machines, the differences were less on average than in those using other technology (*Table 4*). Some observers have argued that accessible voting systems should not be limited to use by voters with disabilities, because that would provide a way for election officials to determine the ballot choices made by that class of voters; it would therefore deprive them of the same degree of ballot secrecy that other voters have.

Influence of Stakeholders on the Acquisition of Voting Systems

Most LEOs play a role in decisions on what voting systems to use in their jurisdictions (see *Table 2* above). Many other stakeholders may also influence those decisions. To help provide an understanding of how LEOs assess the appropriateness of the roles other stakeholders play, the survey asked respondents to what extent they agreed or disagreed with statements about the influence of those stakeholders on the decision-making process. Two examples are "The federal government has too great an influence," and "Local level, elected officials should have greater influence."

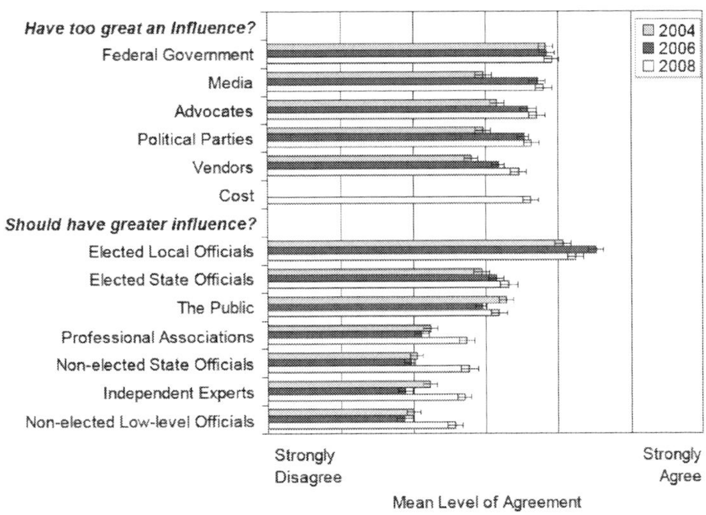

Source: Analysis by CRS of data from capstone surveys.
Note: LEOs were asked about cost only in 2008.

Figure 14. Reactions of LEOs to Statements about the Influence of Various Stakeholders on Decisions about Selection of Voting Systems.

Leos Believed that Several Groups Have too Great an Influence on the Acquisition of Voting Systems, Including the Federal Government, the Media, Advocates, Political Parties, and Vendors, and that Local Elected Officials Have too Little Influence

The results are presented in Figure 14. On average, in fact, LEOs felt more strongly about the role of local elected officials than any other stakeholder. LEOs were largely neutral about the level of influence of state election officials and the public, and did not believe that nonelected officials, professional associations, and independent experts should have greater influence than they do now.

Leos Have Become More Concerned about the Influence of the Media, Political Parties, Advocacy Groups, and Vendors, and More Supportive of Influence by Professionals, Experts, and Nonelected State and Local Officials

Some of the differences among the surveys are notable. As Figure 14 shows, in 2004, LEOs were largely neutral about the influence of the media, political parties, and various advocacy groups.[28] In 2006 and 2008, they thought those groups had too much influence. Also, in 2004 LEOs did not believe on average that vendors had too great an influence. That changed in 2006, when most believed that vendor influence was too high, and that number increased again in 2008.

In contrast, in 2008 LEOs were much less convinced than in 2004 and 2006 that professionals, experts, and nonelected state and local officials should *not* have greater influence. Their views did not change significantly on the roles of the federal government, elected state officials, local elected officials, and the public over the three surveys.

In 2008, LEOs were also asked whether cost has too great an influence on the process of selecting voting systems. They agreed on average that it did, and the strength of that view was about the same as for the media, advocates, political parties, and vendors.

Overall, the observed patterns of response are not surprising. Support for greater influence by local elected officials is expected, because LEOs generally either report to elected local officials or are elected themselves. However, for some questions, elected LEOs and appointed ones had somewhat different views. The support of elected LEOs for greater influence by local elected officials was 20% higher than that of appointed LEOs; support for greater influence by state elected officials and the public was 5%-10% higher. Elected LEOs were 20% less supportive of influence by unelected officials, and 5%-10% less supportive of influence by the federal government, professional associations, and independent experts.

The concerns of local officials about the influence of the federal government are well-known in many areas, not just election administration, and many local officials may have resented the HAVA requirements that led to changes in long-used voting systems.[29] The concerns of LEOs about federal influence have not abated, despite improvements in the attitudes of LEOs about HAVA (see "The Help America Vote Act (HAVA): Impacts and Attitudes" below). Also, it is not surprising that LEOs have become more concerned about the roles of stakeholders such as the media, advocates, and political partisans, who are closely associated with the recent controversies about the reliability and security of voting systems.

There has also been debate and uncertainty specifically about the role and influence of voting system manufacturers and vendors in the selection of voting systems by local jurisdictions. Some observers have argued that vendors have undue influence in what voting systems jurisdictions choose. Others believe that such concerns are unwarranted. But little has been known previously of how LEOs actually view vendors and their relationships with them.

The results of the 2004 survey were mixed with respect to the importance of vendors. (These results are from more detailed questions on factors influencing the acquisition of voting systems that were not included in the 2006 or 2008 surveys.)[30] LEOs in 2004 appeared to have high trust and confidence in vendors but did not rate them as being especially influential with respect to decisions about voting systems—a view that changed over the next two surveys. Fewer than 10% in 2004 believed that there was insufficient oversight of vendors by the federal government and states, but about one in six believed that local governments did not exercise enough oversight.

Most jurisdictions using computer-assisted voting reported in 2004 that they had interacted with their voting-system vendors within the last four years.[31] More than 90% of LEOs considered their voting system vendors responsive and the quality of their goods and services to be high.[32] They felt equally strongly that the recommendations of those vendors could be trusted. However, about a fifth of respondents thought that vendors were willing to sacrifice security for greater profit, although 60% disagreed. Also, a quarter felt that vendors were used for too many elements of election administration.[33]

When LEOs were asked in 2004 what sources of information they relied on with respect to voting systems, state election officials received the highest average rating, with about three-quarters of LEOs indicating that they rely on state officials a great deal. Next most important were other election officials, followed by the federal Election Assistance Commission (EAC) and advocates for the disabled. About one-third of LEOs stated that they relied on vendors a great deal, a level similar to their stated reliance on professional associations. Only 2% of LEOs rated vendors higher than any other source, whereas 20% rated state officials highest. Interest groups were rated lower than vendors, and political parties and media received the lowest ratings.

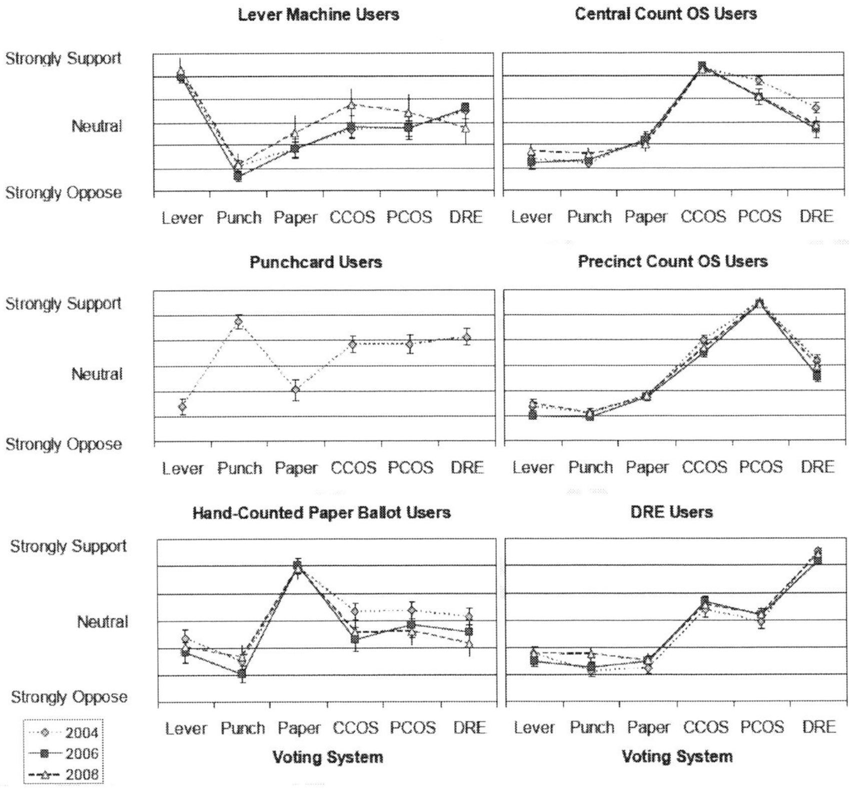

Source: Analysis by CRS of data from capstone surveys.

Note: The X-axis variable (Voting System) is categorical. The data are presented as line, rather than bar, graphs purely as a visual aid to facilitate comparison. The lines do not denote any relationship among the categories. See note for Figure 11 for an explanation of types of voting systems. Each of the six graphs presents the views of LEOs who primarily use the particular kind of voting system denoted on the graph. Data on punchcard users is not presented for 2006 or 2008 because fewer than five LEOs reported using them.

Figure 15. Support of LEOs for the Use of Different Kinds of Voting Systems.

When LEOs were asked in 2004 about the amount of influence different actors had on decisions about voting systems, the overall pattern of response was similar to that for information sources. Once again, state, local, and federal officials were judged the most influential,[34] and political parties and the media the least, with vendors in between. An exception was that local nonelected officials were considered less influential on average than vendors. Both voters and advocates for the disabled were rated as more influential on average than vendors. No LEOs rated vendors as more influential than any other source.

Those results contrast with the views of LEOs described above about whether the levels of influence of stakeholders were too little or too great in 2004 (Figure 14). Of the three actors considered most influential, LEOs believed that local elected officials should have more influence and the federal government has too much, and they were neutral about state officials. They did not believe on average that those considered least influential should have more influence.

Attitudes toward Voting Systems

Leos Were Highly Satisfied with whatever Voting System They Were Using but Were Less Supportive of Other Kinds of Systems

LEOs had strong opinions about the different kinds of voting systems used in the United States. Those whose jurisdiction used a particular kind of system, whatever it was, supported its use more strongly than any other system (see Figure 15).[35] Thus, users of lever machines strongly supported their use, were fairly neutral about DREs and optical scan systems, and were opposed to the use of punchcard and hand-counted paper ballot systems.

In general, except for those using them, LEOs opposed the use of lever machines, punchcard systems, and paper ballots; supported the use of optical scan systems; and were neutral about DREs.[36] Those views changed little across the three surveys. However, support of nonusers for DREs declined across the three surveys, from supportive to neutral. For other voting systems, the levels of preference were fairly consistent.

From 2004 to 2006 there was a slight but significant decrease in the level of support for DREs among users of those systems. DREs were the only voting system for which support of users dropped across the first two surveys, although it still remained very high. It was not possible to determine if the change in support for users of DREs resulted from changes in the views of longtime users or from lower initial support among those who used DREs for the first time in the 2006 election. Whatever the cause, the decline reversed with the 2008 survey.

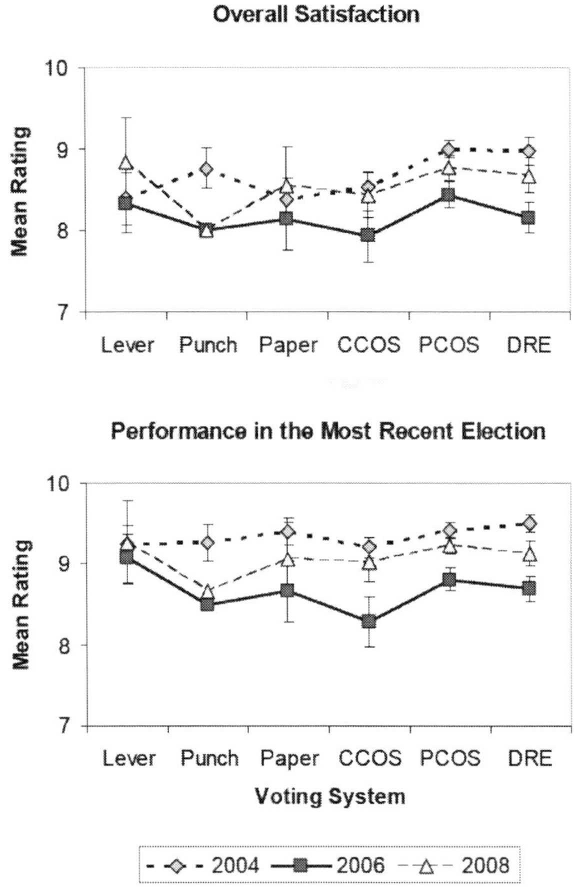

Source: Analysis by CRS of data from capstone surveys.

Note: LEOs were asked to rate overall satisfaction on a scale from 0 (not satisfied at all) to 10 (extremely satisfied), and performance from 0 (not well at all) to 10 (extremely well). Note that the scale on the graph is 7-10, not 0-10. The numbers of LEOs using punchcard systems in 2006 and 2008 were too low to calculate meaningful error bars for that voting system. See note for Figure 11 for an explanation of types of voting systems. See also the note for Figure 15 on the use of line graphs.

Figure 16. Overall Satisfaction of LEOs with Their Primary Voting System and with the Performance of the System.

In 2008, LEOs were also asked about their support for vote-by-phone systems, which are used in several states to meet HAVA's accessibility requirements.[37] Overall, three-quarters of LEOs opposed the use of such systems, and under 10% supported their use. However, opposition was not as strong in states using such systems, where about half of LEOs opposed their use and one-quarter supported it. These systems were only recently adopted, and it was not possible to determine to what extent experience with them influenced the attitudes of LEOs toward them.

Satisfaction with the Voting Systems Leos Used Declined from 2004 to 2006 but Rebounded in 2008

Overall, and consistent with the above results, LEOs reported a high level of satisfaction with their voting systems in all three surveys and assessed that the systems performed very well during the election preceding each survey. On a scale of 0-10, average ratings were 8 or higher for each of those questions in all three surveys (*Figure 16*). However, ratings for satisfaction with and performance of all systems except lever machines were significantly lower in 2006 but rebounded in 2008 to levels that were closer to the ratings in 2004. LEOs still rated DREs lower in 2008 than they had in 2004. There was no difference in ratings across the surveys for lever machines in either satisfaction or performance.[38]

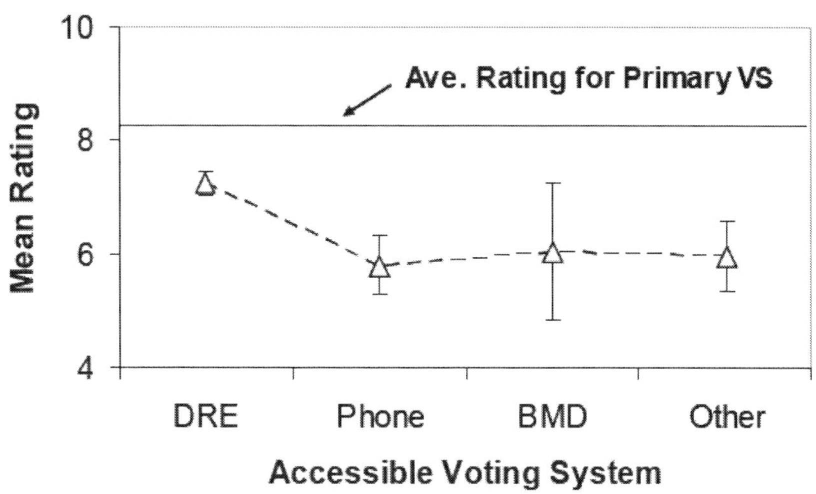

Source: Analysis by CRS of data from capstone surveys.

Figure 17. Overall Satisfaction of LEOs with Their Accessible Voting System, 2008.

In 2008, LEOs were asked to assess their degree of satisfaction with the performance of their accessible voting systems. Those ratings, with an average rating of 6.5 on a scale of 0-10, were lower than the ones for satisfaction with the primary voting system (*Figure 17*). Among the different kinds of accessible system (DRE, ballot-marking device, vote-by-phone, and other), users of DREs were the most satisfied, with an average rating of 7.2. However, even LEOs who also used DRE as their primary voting system were less satisfied with their system in its accessibility performance (7.9) than in its overall performance (8.5).

LEOs who used DREs and precinct-count optical scan systems were more satisfied with them in 2004 than LEOs who used lever machines, paper ballots, or central-count optical scan, but in 2006 and 2008, there were no significant differences in satisfaction among users of different voting systems. However, users of PCOS systems were slightly more satisfied overall than users of either CCOS or DRE systems.[39] There were also no significant differences in rated performance of different voting systems in any of the three surveys.

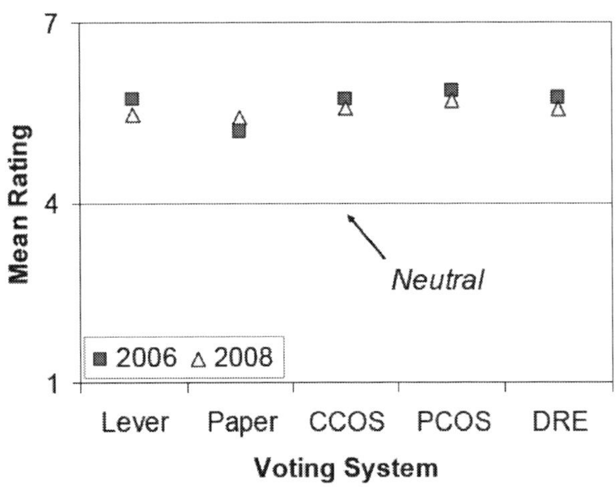

Source: Analysis by CRS of data from capstone surveys.

Note: LEOs were asked how strongly they agreed with the statement, "The voting system in my jurisdiction is the best available," on a scale from 1 (strongly disagree) to 7 (strongly agree). See note for Figure 11 for an explanation of types of voting systems. Data on punchcard users is not presented because only four LEOs reported using them in 2006. For clarity of presentation, confidence intervals are omitted from this graph; they ranged from 0.1 to 0.5.

Figure 18. Average Levels of Agreement among LEOs That Their Current Voting System Is the Best Available, 2006 and 2008.

To assess more directly how LEOs rated their own voting systems in 2006 and 2008, they were asked whether their current system is the best available, and what voting system they believed is best overall. About 80% agreed with the statement that their current voting system is the best available. The level of agreement among users of hand-counted paper ballots was lower than average and that of PCOS users was higher than average (*Figure 18*). The same percentage believed that their current voting system was the best overall in 2006, with a significantly higher percentage of PCOS users holding that view than users of other systems.

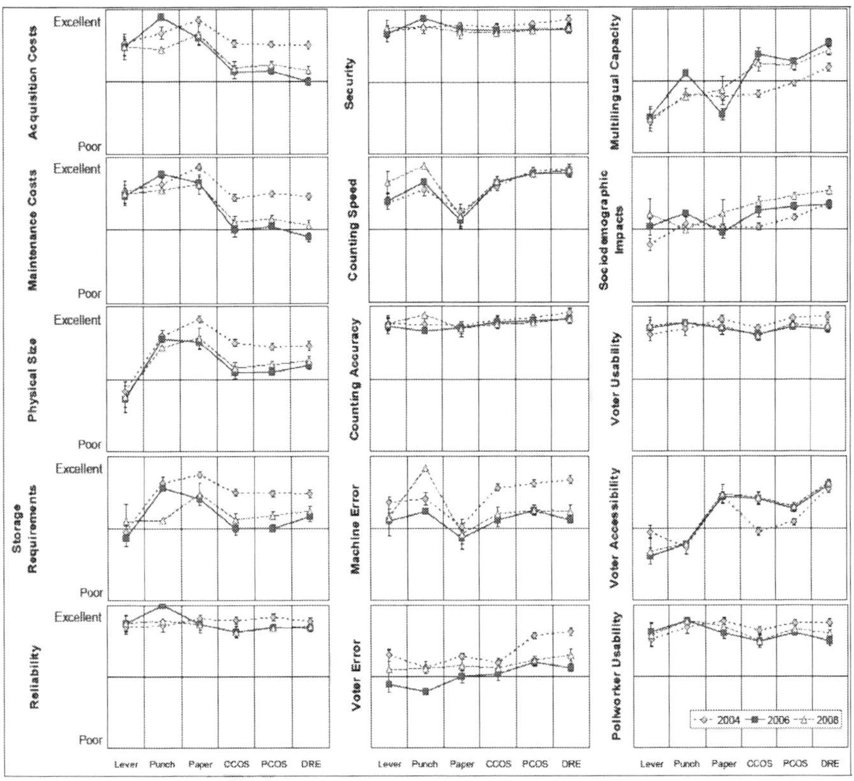

Source: Analysis by CRS of data from capstone surveys.

Note: See note for Figure 11 for an explanation of types of voting systems. See also note for Figure 15. The numbers of LEOs using punchcard systems in 2006 and 2008 were too low to calculate meaningful error bars for that voting system.

Figure 19. Characteristics of the Primary Voting System.

In 2008, LEOs were asked to rank different types of voting systems in order of preference.[40] Not surprisingly, the highest average preference by far was for the current voting system used in the jurisdiction—about three-quarters of LEOs chose that as their top preference—and the lowest was for Internet voting. More than half of PCOS users chose CCOS as their second preference, and more than half of CCOS users ranked PCOS second.

Leos Rated Their Primary Voting Systems as Very Accurate, Secure, Reliable, and Voter- and Pollworker-Friendly, No Matter what Voting System They Used

To further assess voting system preferences, the surveys asked LEOs to assess their primary voting systems on fifteen specific characteristics (*Figure 19*). The high ratings for accuracy, security, reliability, and usability varied little among the different kinds of voting systems in each survey and changed little across the three surveys. Ratings for usability were slightly lower in 2006 and 2008 than in 2004, although those for multilingual capacity, which is a component of usability, were higher.

As the figure shows, for other characteristics, there were substantial differences in many cases both among voting systems in a survey and for a given voting system across the surveys. For most of those characteristics, LEOs were less happy with the performance of their voting system in 2006 and 2008 than in 2004, especially with respect to optical scan and DRE systems, which they rated lower for cost, size, storage requirements, and machine error in the second and third surveys.

Optical scan systems, both central- and precinct-count, were rated higher for accessibility in 2006 and 2008 than in 2004. The reasons for this change are not clear.[41] All systems were rated poorer for machine and voter error in 2006 and 2008—LEOs switched from positive to more neutral about these performance characteristics.

It was not surprising that DREs received the highest ratings of any system for accessibility and ability for use in multiple languages, or that hand-counted paper ballots were rated lowest for counting speed. Some of the comparisons among voting systems, however, did yield surprising results. In particular, the ratings for reliability, security, accuracy, and ease of use by voters were very high and were similar for all voting systems.

Given media reports about problems with the reliability and security of electronic voting, somewhat different outcomes might have been expected—namely, that DREs would have been rated lower in reliability and security. Also, given that modern DREs are often described as more voter-friendly than other systems, and certainly have the capability of providing higher levels of usability than other types, the lack of difference in ratings for usability is somewhat surprising.

With respect to accuracy, a lower rating might have been expected for punchcards, given the difficulties with recounts that were prominent during the 2000 presidential election. It is possible that such confidence exists because few jurisdictions use punch cards now, and those that still use them declined to replace them after 2000. Those jurisdictions kept the system, despite intense negative media coverage of system limitations, and opted not to take part in the punchcard buyout program offered through HAVA.

The relative lack of difference in ratings of optical scan and DRE systems for acquisition and maintenance costs, and size and storage requirements, appears to run counter to widely held views. Many observers regard DREs as the most expensive voting systems, given that several machines may be needed for each polling place, whereas optical scan systems usually require one machine per polling place (PCOS) or none (CCOS).

These differences from expectation suggest that LEOs' perceptions of how their voting systems perform may differ substantially in some ways from views about those systems that have often been depicted by the news media and activists. If the perceptions of election officials are accurate, then several of the criticisms leveled at specific voting systems could lead, if acted upon, to unnecessary and even counterproductive regulation and expenditure. For example, if in fact there is little difference in security between an optical scan system and a DRE, then the requirements for voter-verified paper records of votes that many states have imposed may be unnecessary. If, however, LEOs' perceptions are inaccurate, then understanding and addressing the causes of those inaccuracies may be beneficial. Unfortunately, the survey data do not permit an assessment of which interpretation is correct.

Electronic Voting

Much of the recent controversy about election reform has focused on electronic voting systems. Questions about the security and reliability of those systems were a relatively minor issue until 2003. Two factors led to a sharp increase in public concerns about them: (1) HAVA promoted the use of both PCOS and DREs through its provisions on preventing voter error and making voting systems accessible to persons with disabilities; and (2) the security vulnerabilities of electronic voting systems, especially DREs, were widely publicized as the result of several studies released beginning in 2003.[42]

The surveys asked several questions designed to elicit the views of LEOs about aspects of that controversy. When asked in 2006 whether current federal and state guidelines and standards about electronic voting systems (both optical scan and DRE systems) are at the right degree of strictness, most LEOs—about 60%—replied in the affirmative. Those who did not were fairly evenly split among officials who believed that the current standards are too strict and those who believed they were not strict enough. There was no significant difference in the average assessment between users and nonusers of electronic voting systems, but nonusers were slightly more likely than users to believe that the standards were either too strict or not strict enough (*Figure 20*).

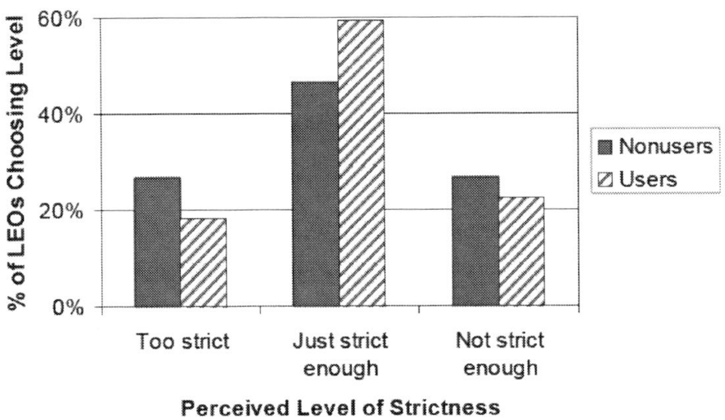

Source: Analysis by CRS of data from capstone surveys.

Note: LEOs were asked, "Do you believe that the state and federal standards for electronic voting systems are too strict or not strict enough?" using a scale from -5 (too strict) to 0 (just strict enough) to 5 (not strict enough). The three categories in the graph show the summed percentages who chose -5 to -1, 0, and 1 to 5, respectively. This question was asked only in 2006.

Figure 20. Assessment by Users and Nonusers of Electronic Voting Systems of the Strictness of Standards for Those Systems, 2006.

DRE Users Differed More from Nonusers in Their Views about Their Voting System than Optical Scan Users Differed from Nonusers

In all three surveys, LEOs were asked to what extent they agreed with several statements about DRE and optical scan systems. In 2004 those questions were asked of all LEOs, but in later surveys they were asked only of those who used DREs and optical scan as their primary voting systems. Also, two questions asked in 2004 were not asked in 2006 (see *Figure 21* and *Figure 22*).

Not surprisingly, the opinions of nonusers of either kind of system were generally less strong than those of users. Nonusers were neutral on average with respect to several statements about DREs, including their level of knowledge about the systems, vulnerability to tampering, and the need for more public trust.

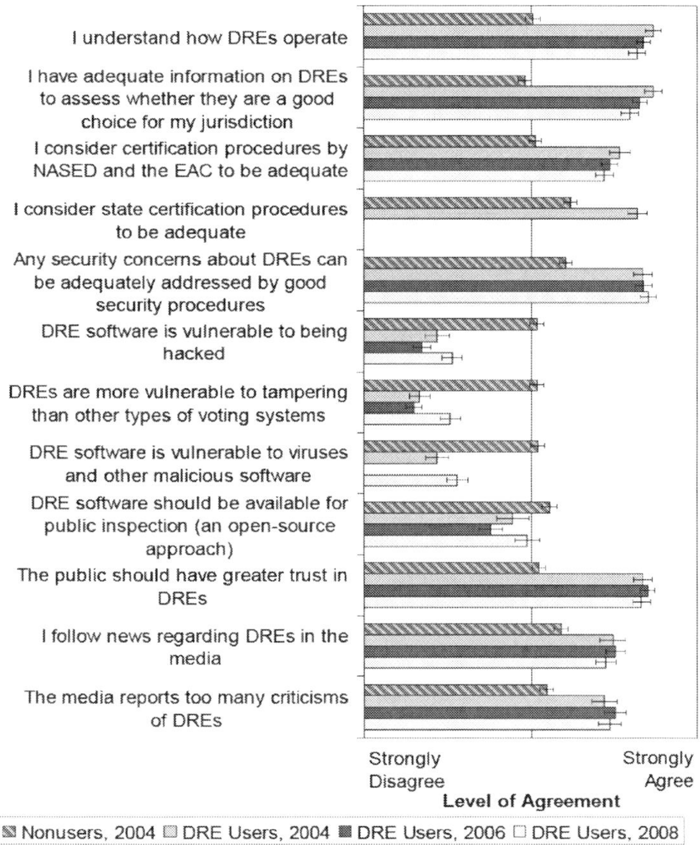

Source: Analysis by CRS of data from capstone surveys.

Note: See text for explanation of the question. Note that not all questions were asked each year.

Figure 21. Views of DRE Users and Nonusers about DREs.

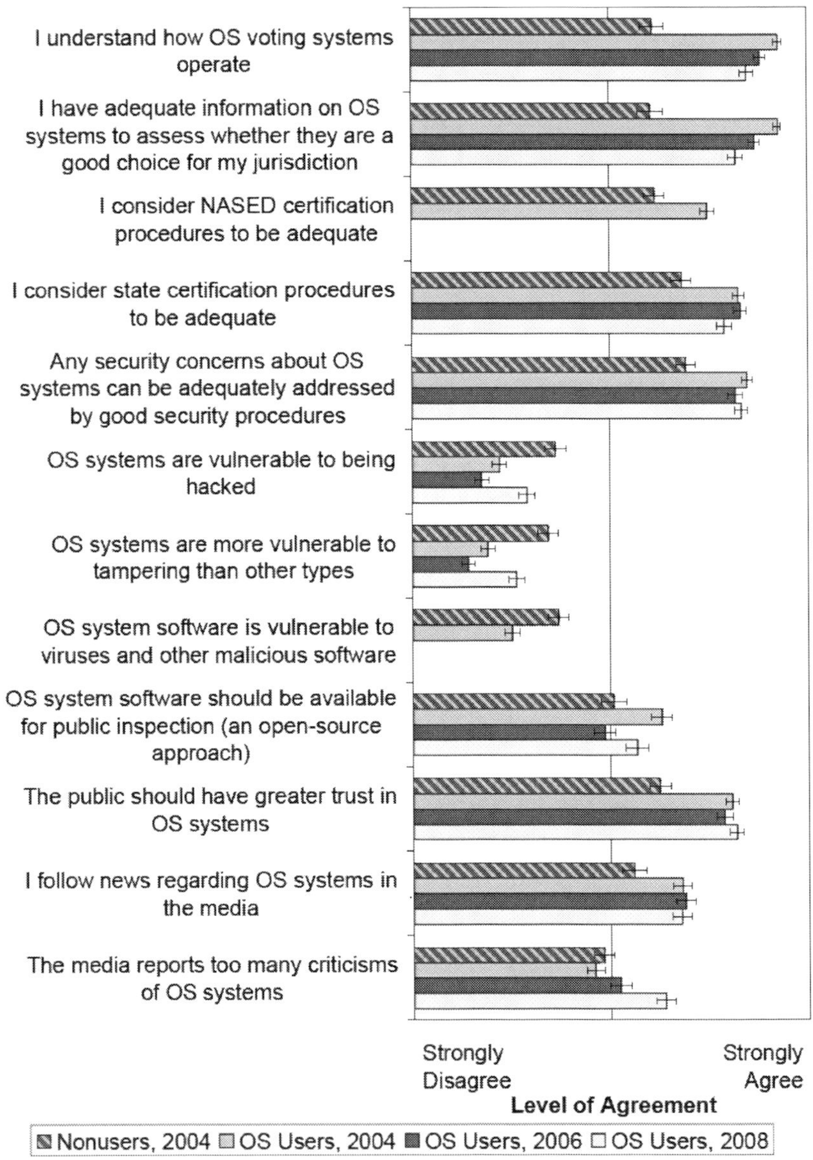

Source: Analysis by CRS of data from capstone surveys.

Note: See text for explanation of the question. Note that not all questions were asked each year.

Figure 22. Views of Users and Nonusers of Optical Scan (OS) Voting Systems About OS Systems.

LEOs whose primary voting systems were precinct-count optical scan were more neutral about DREs than were users of other voting systems.[43] Users of DREs, in contrast, generally agreed that they had sufficient knowledge about the voting system, that certification procedures were adequate, that DREs are not vulnerable to tampering and security concerns can be addressed with good procedures, that the public should have greater trust in DREs, and that the media report too many criticisms of that voting system. Those views were similar in both surveys.

Nonusers were less neutral about optical scan (OS) systems, but users nevertheless held stronger views than nonusers about these systems, except for the statement about media criticism, about which both users and nonusers were neutral on average in 2004. User beliefs about the media were similarly neutral in 2006, but in 2008, they believed that the media were overly critical. LEOs whose primary voting systems were DREs were less neutral about OS systems than users of other voting systems.[44]

The controversy about the security and reliability of DREs has led to widespread calls for the adoption of a paper trail of the ballot choices that a voter can verify before casting the ballot. These paper trails, printed as separate ballot records that the voter can examine, are usually called voter-verified paper audit trails, or VVPAT. LEOs whose primary voting system is a DRE were asked several questions in the surveys about VVPAT. The percentage who used them increased from 18% in 2004 to 36% in 2006 and 46% in 2008.[45] In 2006, about 36% of LEOs whose jurisdictions used DREs as their primary voting system stated that voters who did not wish to use a DRE had the option of using a paper ballot instead. That number increased to 44% in 2008. However, it was not possible to determine which of those jurisdictions permitted that choice in the polling place rather than through the use of "no excuse" absentee balloting.[46]

Given concerns about the auditability of ballots recorded on DREs, users of DREs and OS systems were also asked in 2008 whether they agreed that in close elections the system they used was more open to questions about accuracy than other systems. DRE users were neutral on average about that statement, but OS users disagreed.

About 100 LEOs reported in 2008 that they had recently switched from DREs to another voting system, mostly PCOS. About half of those who switched were more satisfied with their current than their previous voting system, a quarter preferred the DREs, and the rest were neutral about the switch. The most common reasons given for the change were a mandate from the state and the lack of a paper ballot with DREs.

Most LEOS Who Did Not Use Dres Believed that VVPAT Should Be Required, but Most DRE Users Disagreed

About two-thirds of LEOs who did not use DREs supported a VVPAT requirement in 2004 and 2008, [47] whereas one-third or fewer of users did.

Support for VVPAT Increased among DRE Users over the Three Surveys

Fewer than one in five LEOs who used DREs in 2004 believed they should have VVPAT. That number increased to one in three in 2008. The views of nonusers, however, did not change (*Figure 23*)

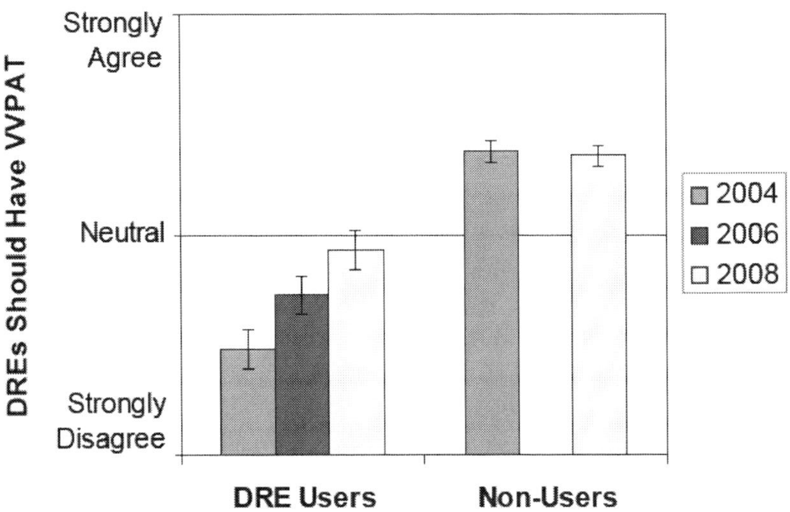

Source: Analysis by CRS of data from capstone surveys.
Note: In the 2006 survey, only DRE users were asked if VVPAT should be required.

Figure 23. Support for VVPAT Among Users and Nonusers of DREs.

The views of DRE users varied depending on whether the machines used VVPAT (*Figure 24*). Not surprisingly, LEOs who used DREs with VVPATs were more supportive of them than other DRE users, except in 2004, when there was no significant difference between the two groups.

In 2006 and 2008, LEOs were also asked if they would be willing to use a VVPAT if reimbursed for the costs by the federal government, and about 60% answered in the affirmative. However, even those respondents (DRE users and nonusers) who expressed support for VVPAT in 2006 were generally willing (65%) to spend only $300 or less for the feature.

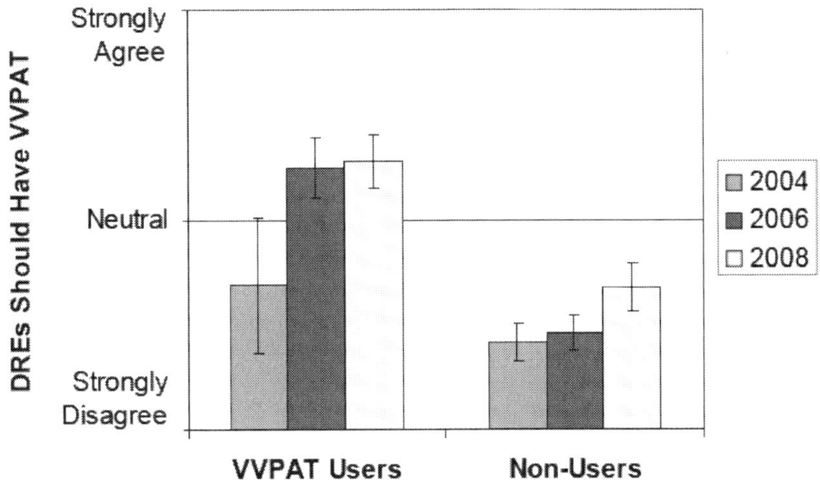

Source: Analysis by CRS of data from capstone surveys.

Figure 24. Support for VVPAT Among Users of DREs With and Without VVPAT.

LEOs were asked to choose one or more of several reasons for disagreeing or agreeing that DREs should produce a VVPAT. The results for DRE users are presented in *Figure 25*. The most frequent reasons chosen varied across the surveys, but the risk of printer failure, the complexity of implementation, and risks to voter privacy were consistently among the most frequently chosen disadvantages, with about half of DRE users choosing them on average. Those LEOs appeared least concerned about risks of tampering. The degree of concern about potential disadvantages was highest in the 2006 survey and lowest in 2008. Only about one-third of LEOs chose any of the three potential advantages listed for this question in the 2006 and 2008 surveys—recounts, checks on accuracy, and improved voter confidence.

DRE users and nonusers differed strikingly in their views on the disadvantages and benefits of VVPAT. In 2008, DRE users expressed far greater concern about the disadvantages and far less agreement with the potential advantages than did nonusers (*Figure 26*). The only exception was that neither group believed on average that risk of tampering was a significant concern in 2008. That was not the case in 2004, when concerns about tampering among users had been four times as high as among nonusers, consistent with differences in views for other potential disadvantages in that survey.[48]

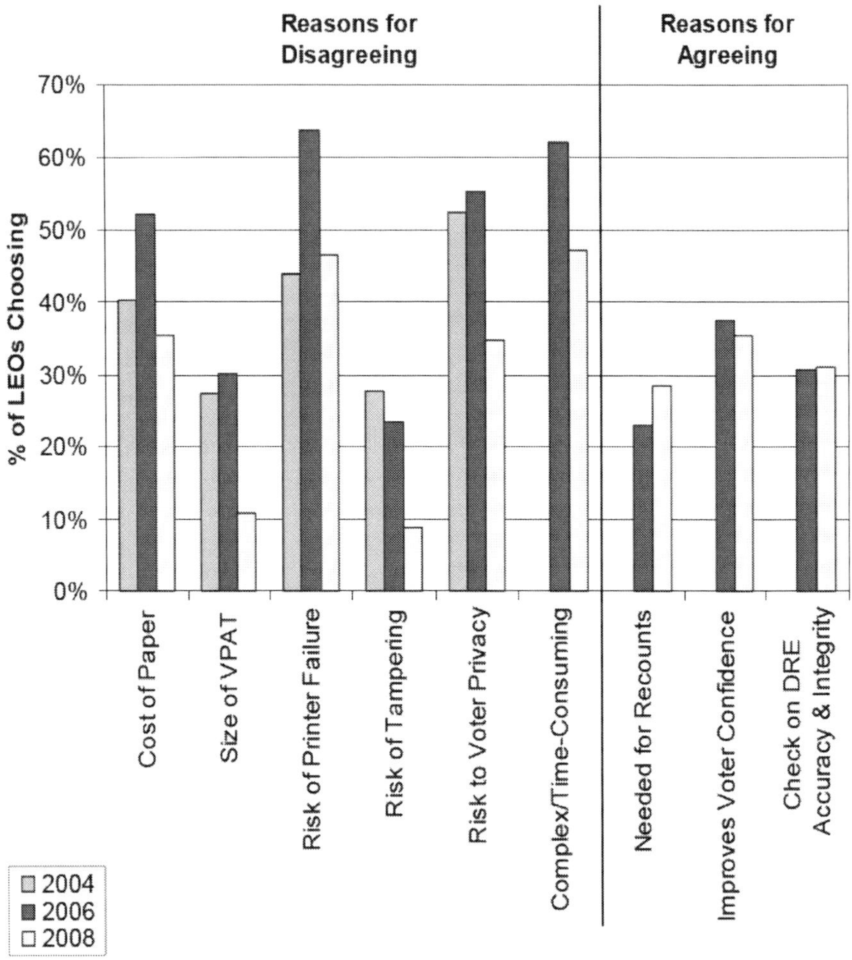

Source: Analysis by CRS of data from capstone surveys.

Figure 25. Reasons Chosen by DRE Users for Disagreeing or Agreeing That DREs Should Print a VVPAT.

In 2008, LEOs with experience using VVPATs were less likely to express concerns about their disadvantages than were other DRE users, and were more likely to agree with the potential advantages (*Figure 27*). Their views were closer to those of LEOs who did not use DREs (*Figure 26*).

Most VVPAT Users Were Satisfied with Them

About three-quarters of LEOs who used a VVPAT were somewhat to very satisfied with it. About one-fifth were dissatisfied in 2006, and fewer than one in ten in 2008. More than four-fifths of LEOs had confidence in the accuracy of VVPAT, with fewer than one-tenth expressing concerns. More than two-thirds thought that voters reacted positively to them in 2006, but only half in 2008 (*Figure 28*).

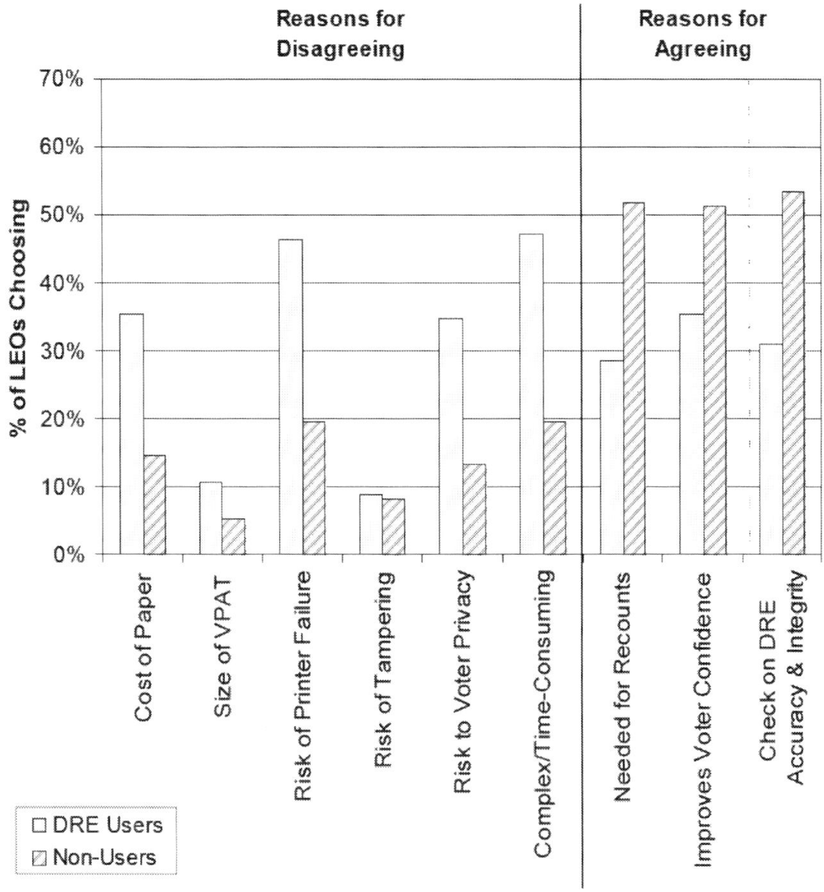

Source: Analysis by CRS of data from capstone surveys.

Figure 26. Reasons Chosen by DRE Users and Non-Users in 2008 for Disagreeing or.Agreeing That DREs Should Print a VVPAT.

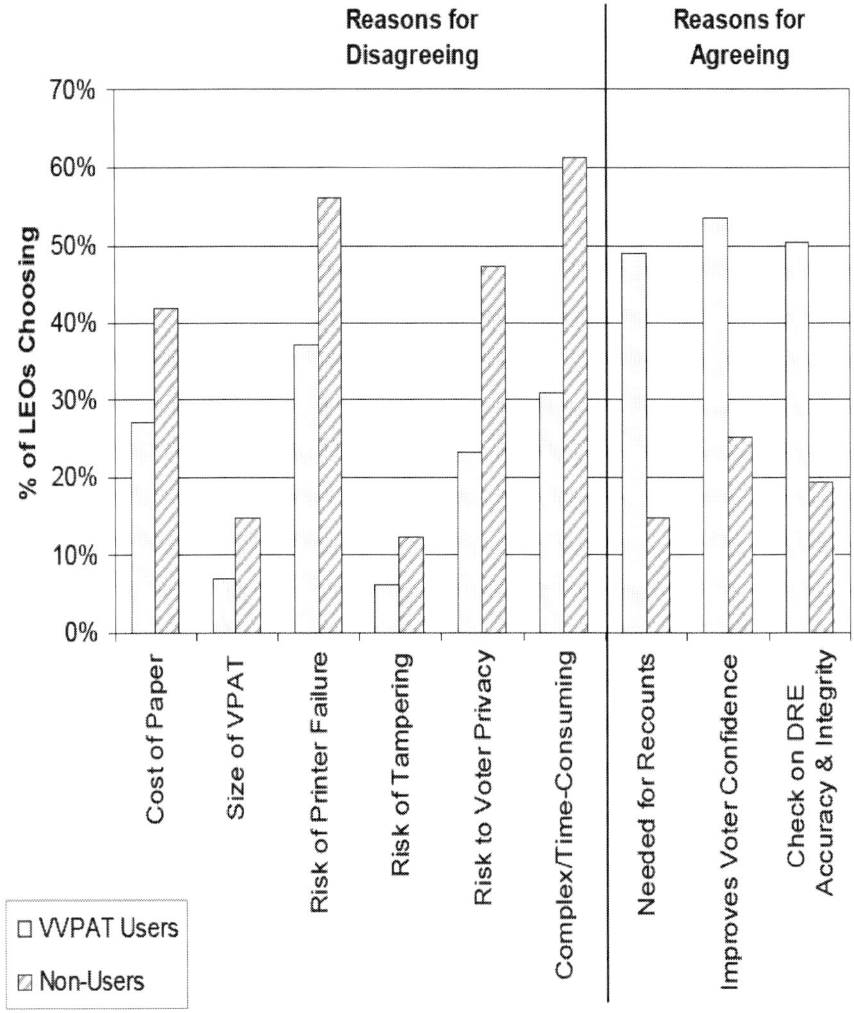

Source: Analysis by CRS of data from capstone surveys.

Figure 27. Reasons Chosen by VVPAT Users and Non-Users in 2008 for Disagreeing or Agreeing That DREs Should Print a VVPAT.

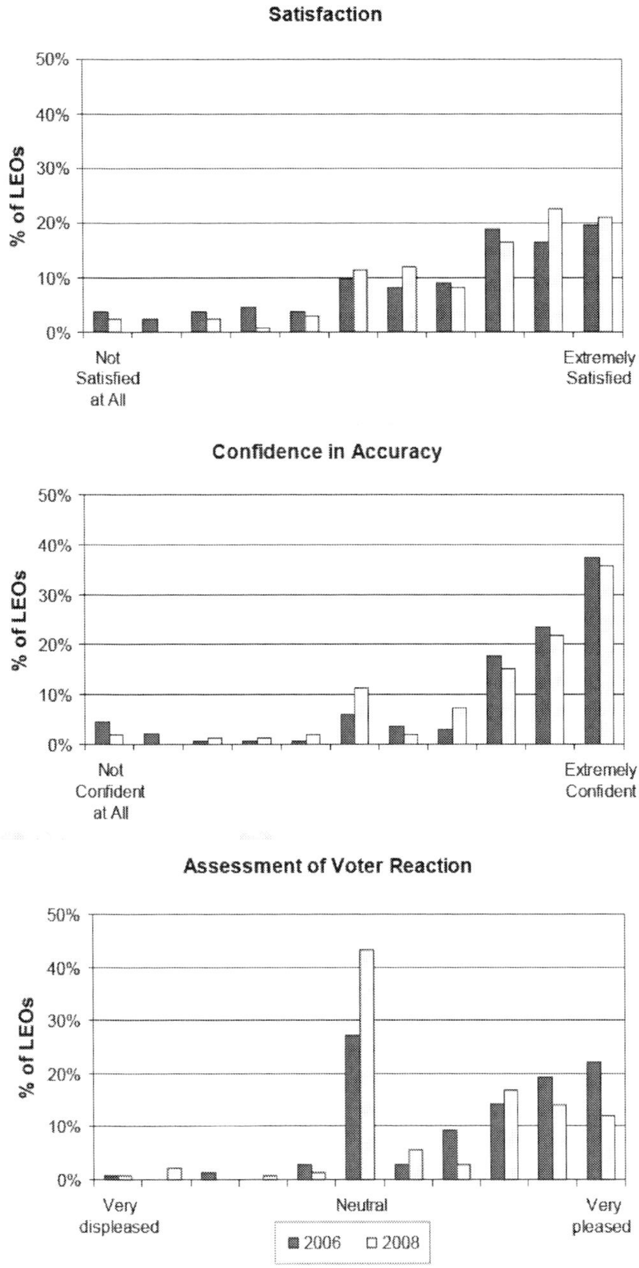

Source: Analysis by CRS of data from capstone surveys.

Figure 28. Reactions to VVPAT by Users, 2006 and 2008.

The Help America Vote Act (HAVA): Impacts and Attitudes

Most LEOs, about 90%, considered themselves familiar with and knowledgeable about HAVA's requirements in the surveys. Those who were "not familiar at all" with HAVA decreased from 4% in 2004 to less than 0.1% in 2008. About 90% of respondents believed that almost all jurisdictions in their state were in full compliance with HAVA provisions in 2006.[49]

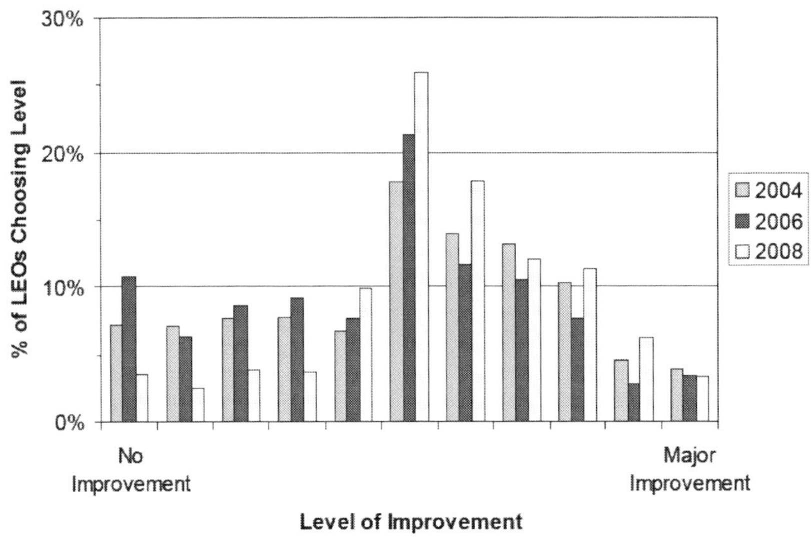

Source: Analysis by CRS of data from capstone surveys.

Figure 29. Assessment by LEOs of Whether HAVA Is Improving the Election Process in Their Jurisdictions.

Leos Believed that HAVA Is Making Moderate Improvements in the Electoral Process Overall in Their Jurisdictions

The strength of this view varied somewhat across the surveys (*Figure 29*). The most favorable assessment was in 2008, and the least favorable in 2006. Also, in the first two surveys, about twice as many LEOs believed that the law resulted in no improvements than in major improvements, but the percentage choosing "no improvement" fell by more than half in 2008, while the percentage choosing "major improvement" was unchanged.

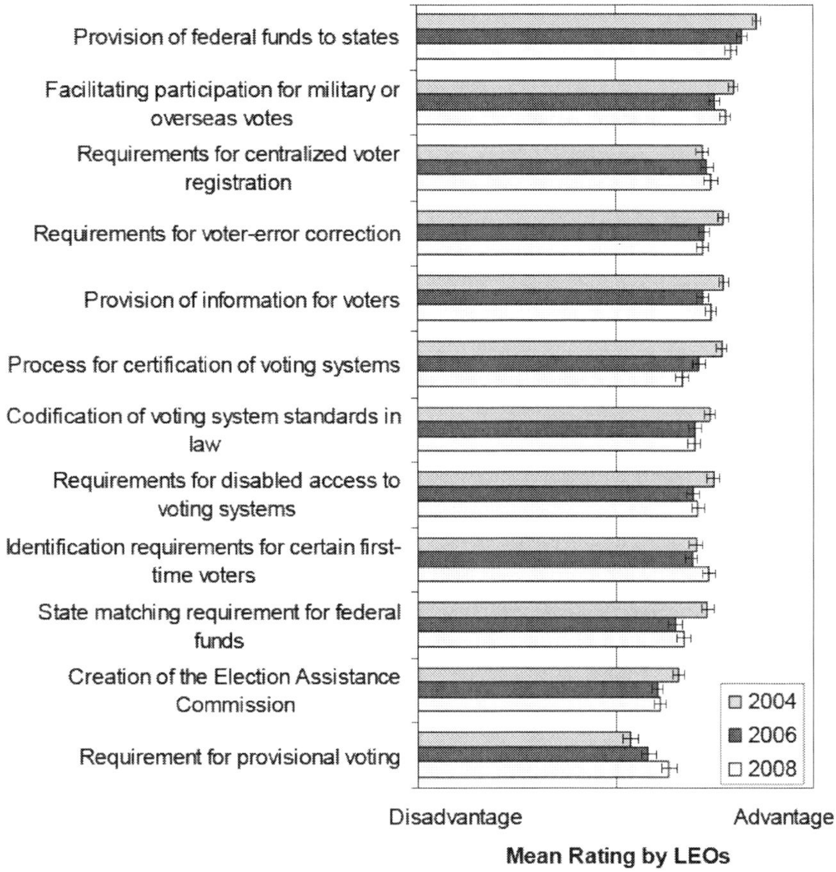

Source: Analysis by CRS of data from capstone surveys.

Figure 30. Assessment of HAVA Provisions as Advantage or Disadvantage.

The views of LEOs in 2008 about the extent to which HAVA had improved elections nationally were similar to their views about local impacts.[50] It might be expected that larger jurisdictions would find HAVA more beneficial than smaller ones, but in fact there was no association between the number of voters in a jurisdiction and how LEOs answered this question. However, the kind of voting system used did have an effect. In each of the surveys, DRE users rated improvements from HAVA highest, followed by users of PCOS, CCOS, and other systems.

Table 5. Assessment by LEOs of Advantageousness of HAVA Provisions

	Percentage of LEOs Choosing Assessment											
	Advantage				Neutral				Disadvantage			
HAVA Provision	2004	2006	2008	Δ	2004	2006	2008	Δ	2004	2006	2008	Δ
Provision of federal funds to states	90	81	81	-9	6	12	13	7	4	7	6	2
Facilitating participation for military or overseas votes	82	72	80	-2	11	18	15	4	7	10	5	-2
Requirements for centralized voter registration	71	70	74	3	16	17	16	0	13	13	10	-3
Requirement for voter-error correction	78	68	69	-9	13	22	24	11	8	11	7	-1
Provision of information for voters	79	67	75	-4	15	25	22	7	5	8	3	-2
Process for certification of voting systems	79	67	64	-15	15	21	21	6	7	13	15	8
Codification of voting system standards in law	74	64	68	-6	19	25	23	4	8	11	9	1
Requirement for disabled access to voting systems	76	64	69	-7	13	18	18	5	11	17	13	2
Identification requirements for certain first-time voters	68	64	73	5	16	20	17	1	16	16	10	-6
State matching requirement for federal funds	74	57	61	-13	14	24	23	9	12	20	15	3
Creation of the Election Assistance Commission	62	48	49	-13	23	31	37	14	15	21	13	-2
Requirement for provisional voting	49	51	58	9	17	20	23	6	35	30	20	-15

Source: Analysis by CRS of data from capstone surveys.

Note: Δ = Change from 2004 to 2008. LEOs we respondents who chose 5-7, for the Neutral column 4, and for the Disadvantage column 1-3..

Leos Supported All Major Provisions of HAVA, but the Degree of Support Changed Across the Surveys

Most LEOs regarded the major provisions of HAVA as advantageous. However, the average level of support varied among both the provisions and the surveys. LEOs were most supportive of federal funding and least supportive of the requirement for provisional voting and the creation of the EAC (Figure 30). Provisional voting received substantially higher negative ratings than any other provision in the surveys, but the proportion of LEOs rating it as a disadvantage declined more than 40% from 2004 to 2008 (Table 5).

While remaining positive overall, the level of support decreased for seven provisions across the surveys, especially from 2004 to 2006. They were provision of federal funds, error-correction requirements, the certification process for voting systems, codification of voting-system standards in law, accessibility requirement, the requirement for state matching funds, and the creation of the EAC. However, even for the EAC, which, along with provisional ballots, had the lowest rating in 2008, half of LEOs regarded it as an advantage and fewer than one in seven as a disadvantage in that survey.

Decreased support for funding might have been caused simply by the decrease in availability of federal funds over the course of the three elections. Controversies about the security and reliability of different voting systems might have contributed to the decline in support for provisions relating to voting systems and the EAC.

There was no significant change for four provisions: facilitating participation for military and overseas voters, the requirement for centralized voter registration, the provision of information to voters, and identification requirements for certain first-time voters. Support for one provision— the requirement for provision voting—actually increased with each survey.

Support for HAVA's provisions also varied to some extent with the primary voting system used in the jurisdiction. DRE users exhibited the strongest support for the requirement on accessibility, provisional ballots, and military and overseas voters, and for the codification of standards. DRE and PCOS users expressed the strongest support for the error correction requirement.

Users of hand-counted paper ballots exhibited lower support than users of other systems for the provisions on federal funding, provisional ballots, facilitation of military and overseas voting, and the codification of standards.

Nevertheless, all were regarded as advantages except provisional ballots, toward which users of paper ballots were neutral on average.

Leos Perceived HAVA Provisions as Moderately Difficulty to Implement

In general, LEOs reported in all three surveys that implementation of HAVA provisions was moderately difficult (Figure 31). The level of difficulty for three provisions declined from 2004 to 2008: provisional voting, accessibility, and provision of information for voters. For one, the process for certification of voting systems, the reported difficulty of implementation increased.[51]

The other provisions exhibited no net change, although for voter identification and error correction, the perceived difficulty was lower in 2006 than in the presidential election years.

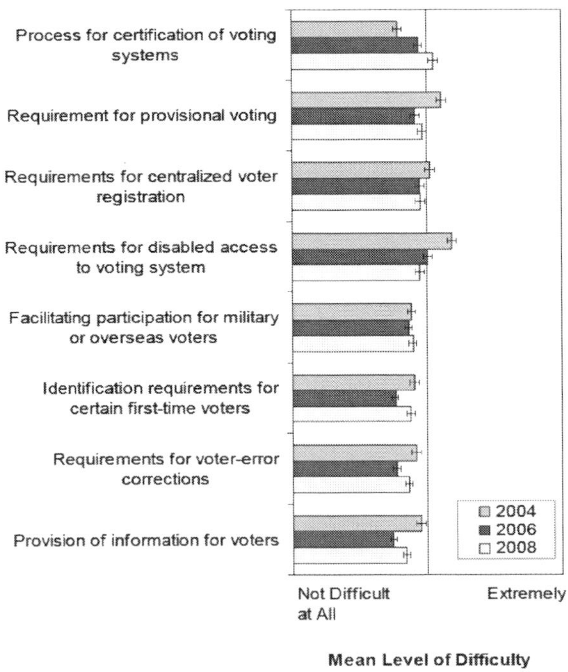

Source: Analysis by CRS of data from capstone surveys.

Figure 31. Perceived Level of Difficulty by LEOs in Implementing HAVA Provisions.

Not surprisingly, LEOs were less likely to support a provision they found difficult to implement. That is, there was an inverse relationship between the reported level of difficulty and the reported advantageousness of a provision. That pattern held for all provisions, but was most pronounced for provisional ballots, and least for the provision of information to voters.

Users of Different Voting Systems Varied in How Difficult They Found Provisions to Implement

Optical scan users found the accessibility requirement more difficult than did users of other voting systems. Perhaps surprisingly, DRE users did not find this provision significantly less difficult to implement than did users of hand-counted paper ballots, punch cards, or lever machines.

PCOS and DRE users found the voter error-correction requirement easier to implement than did users of other voting systems. That finding is consistent with the greater error prevention and correction features of those systems, although lever machines also possess error prevention features.

Users of paper ballots perceived the certification provision as less difficult to implement than users of other systems, as would be expected, given the acquisition of certified voting systems would likely be less important for them than for users of optical scan and DRE systems and lever machines in the process of being replaced. However, it is not clear why PCOS users reported similar levels of difficulty for that provision. Similarly, it is not clear why CCOS users found the voter registration requirement more difficult to implement than did users of other voting systems. Users of different kinds of systems did not differ in their assessments of the difficulty of implementing the provisions on military and overseas voters, provisional ballots, and voter identification.

Most Leos Reported that HAVA Has Increased the Cost of Elections, and They Are Concerned about Future Funding

The decrease in support for most HAVA provisions across the three surveys may have resulted in part from perceptions about costs and funding. The importance of these factors is also supported by the responses to three questions in the 2006 and 2008 surveys:

- How has HAVA affected the cost of elections in your jurisdiction?
- To what degree is the funding your jurisdiction has received to implement HAVA requirements sufficient for their implementation?
- How concerned are you that limited funding in the future will leave you unable to comply with HAVA requirements for election administration?

The results are presented in *Figure 32.*

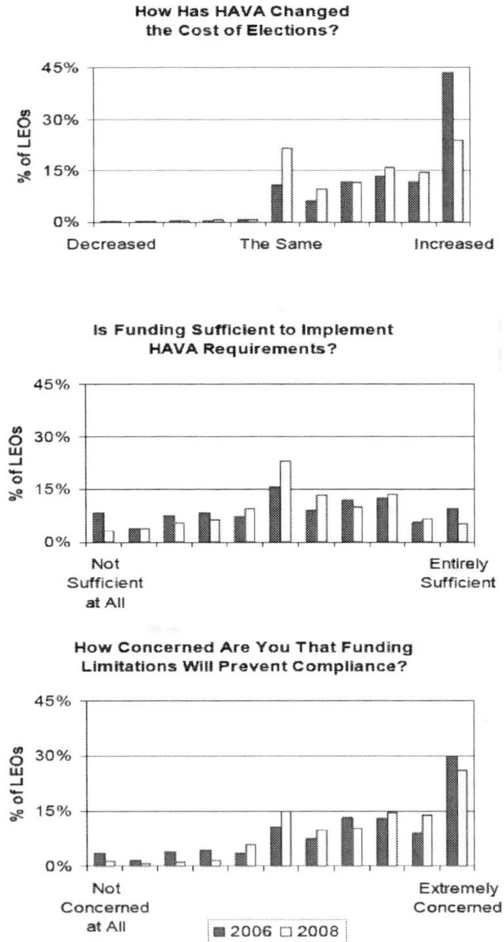

Source: Analysis by CRS of data from capstone surveys.

Figure 32. Response of LEOs to Questions about Funding Effects of HAVA, 2006 and 2008.

About 90% of respondents in 2006 and 75% in 2008 believed that HAVA has increased the cost of elections, and only 2% believed the costs have decreased. LEOs were fairly evenly divided in both surveys on whether current funding is sufficient to implement the requirements, but most expressed concerns about the sufficiency of future funding, with 25%-30% stating that they were "extremely concerned." LEOs were also concerned about the impact on election administration of the financial crisis that arose in 2008, with more than 60% indicating that they were moderately to very concerned, and only 4% reporting that they were not concerned at all.

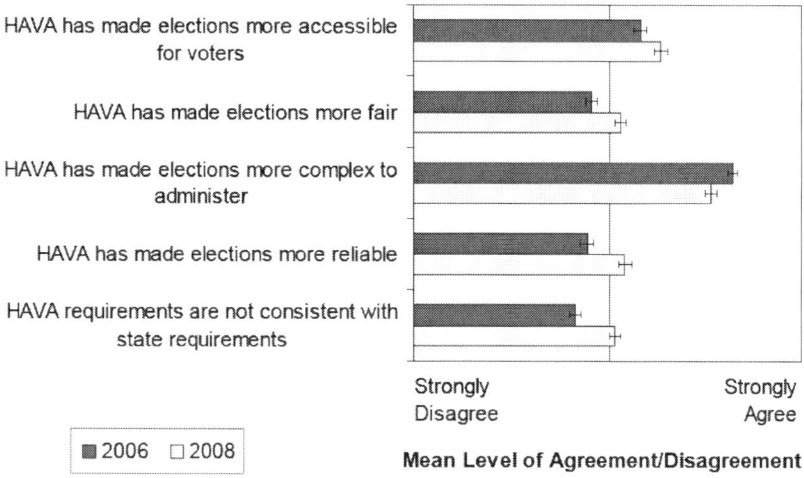

Source: Analysis by CRS of data from capstone surveys.

Figure 33. Reactions of LEOs to Statements about the Impacts of HAVA, 2006 and 2008.

Leos Reported in 2008 that HAVA Has Improved the Accessibility, Fairness, and Reliability of Elections but Has Made Them More Complicated to Administer

LEOs were also asked in 2006 and 2008 to respond to a set of statements about the impacts of HAVA (Figure 33). Their views changed significantly across the two surveys. They agreed on average in both that HAVA has made elections more accessible for voters, and they held that view more strongly in 2008. In 2006, they disagreed that the law has made elections fairer or more reliable, but agreed with those views on average in 2008. In 2006, they did not believe that HAVA requirements were inconsistent with state requirements, and they were neutral on average about that statement in 2008.

Table 6. Distribution of Responses of LEOs to Statements about the Impacts of HAVA, 2006 and 2008

Statement	Percentage of LEOs Who…					
	Disagreed		Were Neutral		Agreed	
	2006	2008	2006	2008	2006	2008
HAVA has made elections more accessible for voters	26%	16%	23%	24%	51%	60%
HAVA has made elections more fair	40%	24%	31%	40%	30%	36%
HAVA has made elections more complex to administer	7%	8%	8%	14%	85%	78%
HAVA has made elections more reliable	42%	24%	28%	37%	29%	39%
HAVA requirements are not consistent with state requirements	44%	23%	33%	47%	23%	30%

Their most strongly held view in both surveys was that HAVA has made elections more complex to administer. As Table 6 shows, responses to the statement on complexity of elections were the least evenly distributed, with about one-quarter to one-half of respondents expressing a neutral position.

Leos Were Skeptical about How Much Attention Congress Pays to Their Views

In 2008, LEOs were asked how much attention they thought Congress will pay to their views when considering legislation regarding election administration. In general, they appeared skeptical that their views would be heard (Figure 34). About one in seven believed that Congress would pay no attention at all, and fewer than 3% believed that a great deal of attention would be paid. It could not be determined whether these views arose from their experiences relating to the development of HAVA or from some other source, such as a more general skepticism about government responsiveness.

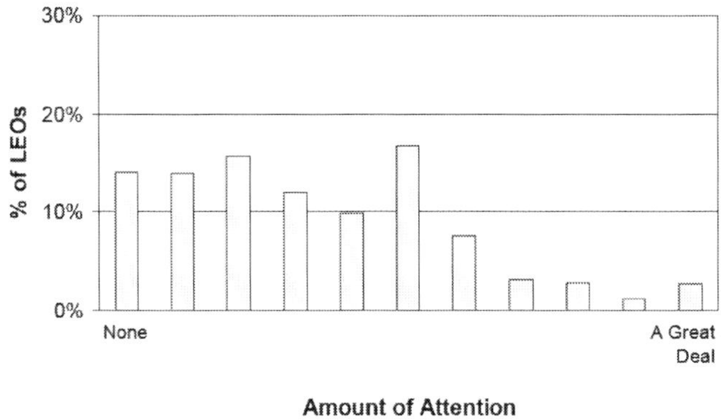

Source: Analysis by CRS of data from capstone surveys.

Figure 34. Assessment by LEOs of How Much Attention Congress Will Pay to Their Views When Considering Legislation on Election Administration, 2008.

Election Assistance Commission

When HAVA created the Election Assistance Commission, the law gave it several specific responsibilities. The EAC carries out grant programs, provides for voluntary testing and certification of voting systems, studies election issues, and issues voluntary guidelines for voting systems and guidance for the requirements in the act. The EAC has no rule-making authority (other than very limited authority under the National Voter Registration Act, the "motor-voter" law, P.L. 103-31) and does not enforce HAVA requirements.

In the 2006 and 2008 surveys, LEOs were asked about the EAC's responsibilities, helpfulness, and benefits. They were asked to rank the importance of the following four EAC responsibilities:

- Provide *guidance* to local election officials,
- *Research* issues related to election administration,
- *Certify* voting systems, and
- Ensure that local jurisdictions are in *compliance* with federal law.

Most Leos Found Most Activities of the EAC Moderately Important

The results are presented in *Figure 35*. LEOs regarded guidance to them as the most important of the listed responsibilities and ensuring compliance by them as the least.[52] Research and certification were rated in the middle, and the ratings for them did not differ significantly. The results were consistent across both surveys. When asked in 2006 how many times the EAC had helped them understand or perform their duties during the previous year, about one third indicated that the EAC had helped at least once, and about 10% ten or more times.[53]

The degree to which LEOs found the EAC helpful improved substantially from 2006 to 2008 (*Table 7*). In 2006, almost half of LEOs had found the EAC not very helpful, with 13% finding it "not helpful at all." In 2008, the proportion of more negative ratings dropped by more than half, with only about one-fifth finding the EAC not very helpful, and only 3% choosing "not helpful at all." The proportion finding the EAC moderately helpful doubled, from about one-third to two-thirds. However, the proportion who found the EAC very helpful did not increase, but remained at about one-fifth.

Table 7. Perceptions of LEOs about the Helpfulness of the EAC, 2006 and 200

Perceived Degree of Helpfulness	2006	2008
Less helpful	46%	18%
Moderately helpful	35%	65%
More helpful	19%	17%

Source: Analysis by CRS of data from capstone surveys.

Notes: LEOs were asked to rate the degree of helpfulness of the EAC to them on a scale of 0 (not helpful at all) to 10 (extremely helpful). In the table, less helpful = 0-3, moderately helpful = 4-6, more helpful = 7-10.

LEOs were also asked how they had benefitted from the four functions listed above plus the distribution of federal funds for use by local jurisdictions. The ratings (*Figure 36*) generally reflect the pattern seen in the responses on overall helpfulness. On average, LEOs responded that they had benefitted only moderately overall, but the average level of benefit for each category was higher in 2008 than in 2006.[54] However, while they considered local guidance as the most important responsibility (see *Figure 35*), they rated it lowest in benefit, along with local compliance, which they regarded as the least important responsibility. About a quarter rated EAC guidance as "not beneficial at all," with about 7% rating it "extremely beneficial." Perceived benefits from research and certification were somewhat higher, and funding, not surprisingly, was rated highest.

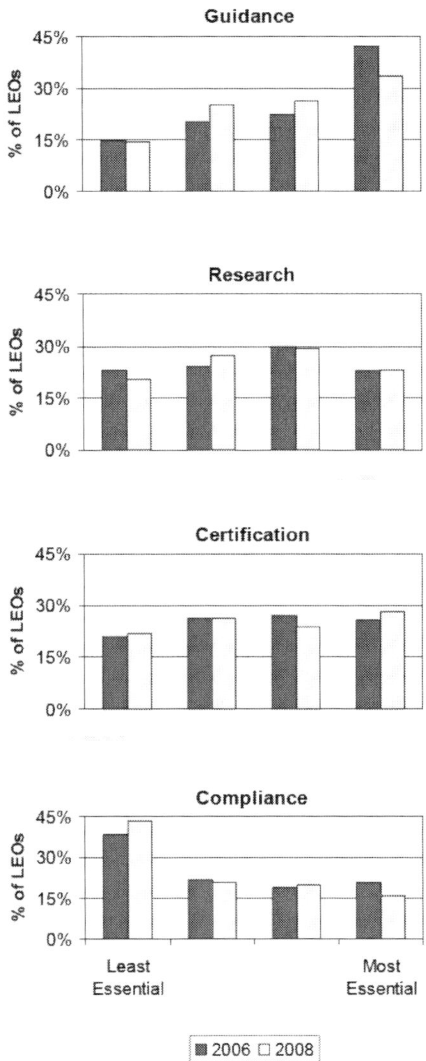

Source: Analysis by CRS of data from capstone surveys.

Figure 35. Perceived Importance by LEOs of Selected EAC Responsibilities, 2006 and 2008.

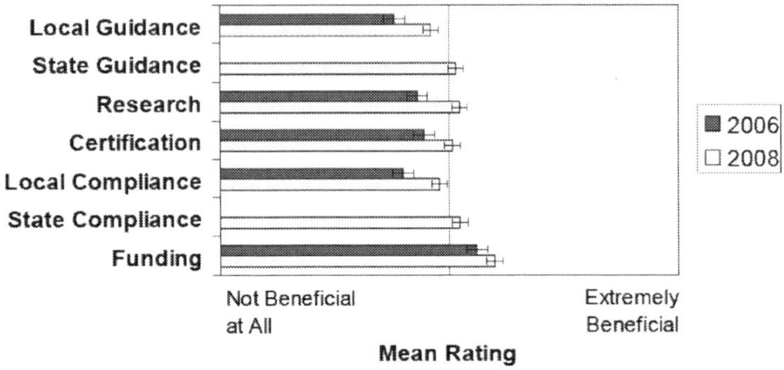

Source: Analysis by CRS of data from capstone surveys.

Figure 36. Perceived Degree of Benefit to LEOs from EAC Functions, 2006 and 2008.

There might be several possible explanations for the discrepancy in the ratings for importance versus benefits of EAC guidance to local jurisdictions. For example, it could reflect frustration with the delays in the initial start-up of the EAC, an explanation that is consistent with the increase in ratings in 2008. It could reflect difficulties in understanding the guidance that the EAC issued. It might reflect the fact that the purpose of the guidance stated in HAVA is to assist states, not local jurisdictions, in meeting the title III requirements (§311(a)). Consistent with that explanation, when LEOs were asked in 2008 about guidance and compliance at the state level, they perceived each of those as being more beneficial than at the local level (*Figure 36*). Or it could simply be an expression of opposition to or uncertainty about the requirements themselves. Individual comments from LEOs in 2006 and 2008[55] suggest a diversity of views about the EAC:

- They need to move faster, the new system or changes to old systems need to get certified in a reasonable amount of time.
- Much of the information received from the EAC either did not apply ... or was already in practice for many years.
- The EAC's information on their website can be very helpful.
- My local jurisdiction does not really see anything from the EAC because the state usually takes care of it and then passes it on to us to comply.
- EAC commissioners and staff are very well aware of their situation and environment. I work closely with them on a regular basis and know they are doing the best they can, as a federal agency with no enforcement powers....

- I would like for the EAC to work more with states to have equipment certified and power to enforce that certification. I also wish the EAC members did not change so often—it takes a long time to learn....
- Exempt cities or other entities with less than 2,000 voters from the very expensive HAVA equipment requirements.
- Get rid of it. Elections ... should be free of federal control.
- I believe they need more power to correct election problems.

Voter Registration Database

HAVA required each state to implement a statewide, computerized voter registration list before the 2006 election. A few states were unable to meet that deadline, and that is reflected in the survey, with 6% of respondents indicating that their states had not yet met the requirement in 2006, and 4% in 2008.[56] Most LEOs were familiar with their state's database, with about a third assessing themselves as "very familiar" in 2006.[57]

Given the concerns expressed in the first survey about the burdens of HAVA implementation, the second survey asked LEOs whether the implementation of the computerized list had required the hiring of additional staff in the local jurisdiction.[58] Four-fifths responded that it had not. Those that did hire additional staff were asked to identify all sources of funds. More than three-quarters received funding from local governments (*Figure 37*), with about 70% receiving *only* local funding.

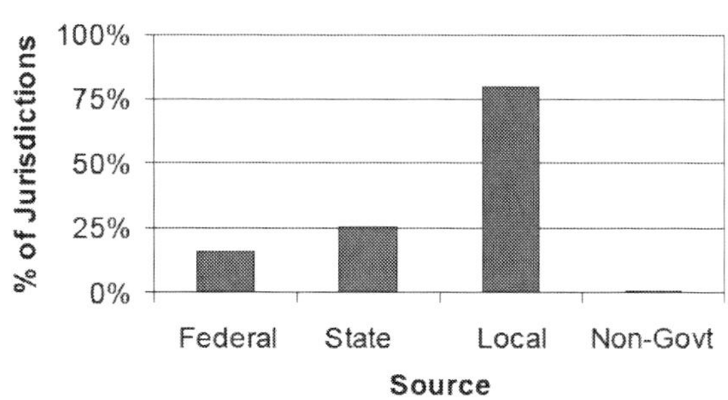

Source: Analysis by CRS of data from capstone surveys.
Note: There were 234 jurisdictions that reported requiring additional staffing in 2006.

Figure 37. Sources of Funds Reported by LEOs for Additional Local Staffing for the Voter Registration Database Required by HAVA, 2006.

Table 8. Levels of Confidence Reported by LEOs in Selected Features of Their Voter Registration Databases, 2006 and 2008

	Contingency Plans	Security		Accuracy
Confidence Rating	2006	2006	2008	2008
Low	6%	1%	1%	2%
Moderate	32%	24%	34%	40%
High	61%	75%	66%	59%

Source: Analysis by CRS of data from capstone surveys.

Notes: LEOs were asked to rate their level of confidence for each item on a scale of 0 (lowest) to 10 (highest).

Entries for Low column include respondents who chose 0-2, for Moderate 3-7, and for High 8-10. The question about security was asked in 2006 and 2008, the one about contingency plans was asked only in 2006, and that about accuracy only in 2008.

To explore perceptions about the effectiveness of the computerized statewide voter registration database, LEOs were asked about security, accuracy, and contingency plans in case of failure on election day.[59] Respondents were very confident about each (*Table 8*).[60]

LEOs were also asked about their agreement or disagreement with a series of statements about the voter registration database. The responses (*Figure 38*) are generally consistent with the responses to the questions on accuracy and security. Most LEOs did not believe that the database could be accessed by unauthorized people or manipulated improperly. They did not believe it created problems for legitimately registered voters, and did not see challenges from political parties and others as a significant problem.

Leos Had More Confidence in the Voter Registration Databases in 2008 than They Had in 2006

They were less concerned about reliability, administrative burden, matching problems, inadvertent removal of voters, and identity theft. Their views on security were unchanged. They continued to believe that the new databases were to some degree an improvement over the previous systems and were somewhat more accurate and fair. They remained neutral on average about whether the new systems would reduce the need for provisional ballots. However, for this statement, although not for any of the others, the number of voters in the jurisdiction had a significant impact. LEOs with larger jurisdictions were more likely to believe that the new databases reduced the need for provisional ballots than were those with small jurisdictions.

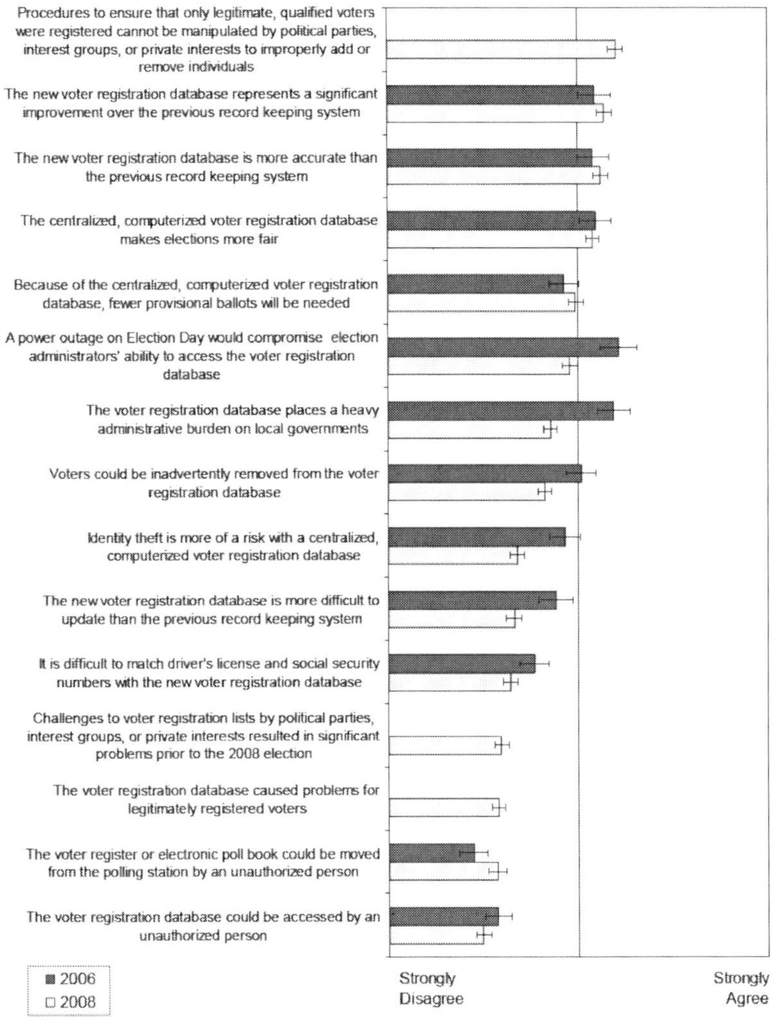

Source: Analysis by CRS of data from capstone surveys.
Note: Sample sizes differed substantially in the two surveys. See text.

Figure 38. Agreement/Disagreement of LEOs with Statements About the Voter Registration Database, 2006 and 2008.

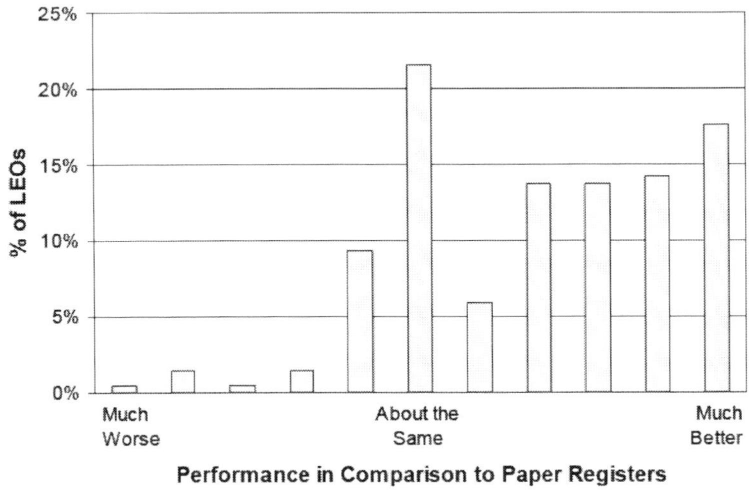

Source: Analysis by CRS of data from capstone surveys.

Figure 39. Assessment by LEOs of the Performance of Electronic Pollbooks in Resolving Issues About Voter Eligibility, 2008.

Most Leos Who Used Electronic Pollbooks Were Positive About Them

In 2008, LEOs were asked about their use of electronic pollbooks, which provide immediate electronic access to the state's voter registration database at the polling place. About one in six

reported that they used them.[61] About two-thirds of those reported that electronic pollbooks were better than paper registers in resolving issues about voter eligibility (*Figure 39*). About 10% considered them worse, and the rest were neutral.

Voter Identification

Issues relating to voter identification have been controversial.[62] HAVA requires that first-time voters who register by mail must present a specified form of identification, either when registering or when voting. The law does not require photographic identification, although a few states have such requirements, and many states require some form of identification document.[63]

About two-thirds of LEOs reported that their jurisdictions required some form of document identification from all voters. About one-third of jurisdictions used signature comparisons. Roughly one-quarter permitted the voter to provide identification verbally via some form of personal information, such as name and address (*Figure 40*).

Leos Supported Requiring Photo Identification for All Voters, Even though They Believed It Would Negatively Affect Turnout and Did Not Believe that Voter Fraud Is a Serious Problem in Their Jurisdictions

One of the principal policy arguments often cited for tightening voter-identification requirements is concern about the risk of significant levels of voting by ineligible voters. Opponents counter that those risks are small and that requiring identification, especially photo IDs, would effectively disenfranchise many eligible voters who would have difficulty obtaining such documents.[64] To help determine the views of LEOs about this issue, the surveys asked several additional questions about voter identification:

- As a local election official, how supportive are you of requiring all voters in your jurisdiction to provide valid photo identification?
- How often do non-eligible persons attempt to vote in your jurisdiction, either in person or by absentee ballot?[65]
- Do you agree or disagree that deliberate voter fraud is a serious problem in your jurisdiction?
- Do you believe that requiring photo identification of all voters would make elections more secure, less secure, or have no impact on election security?
- Do you believe that asking for photo identification of all voters would increase turnout, decrease turnout, or have no impact on turnout?

The results are presented in *Figure 41*. On average, LEOs mildly supported a requirement for photo identification. However, about 30% of respondents chose "extremely supportive," 5%-10% "do not support at all," and the choices of the other 60% were spread across the scale of possible responses. LEOs whose jurisdictions used hand-counted paper ballots were somewhat less supportive of photo ID than other jurisdictions, perhaps because those jurisdictions had many fewer voters on average than other jurisdictions (see *Figure 49* below), and those LEOs therefore might be more likely to know voters personally. DRE users, who tended to have large jurisdictions, were more supportive on average of photo ID than were users of other systems.

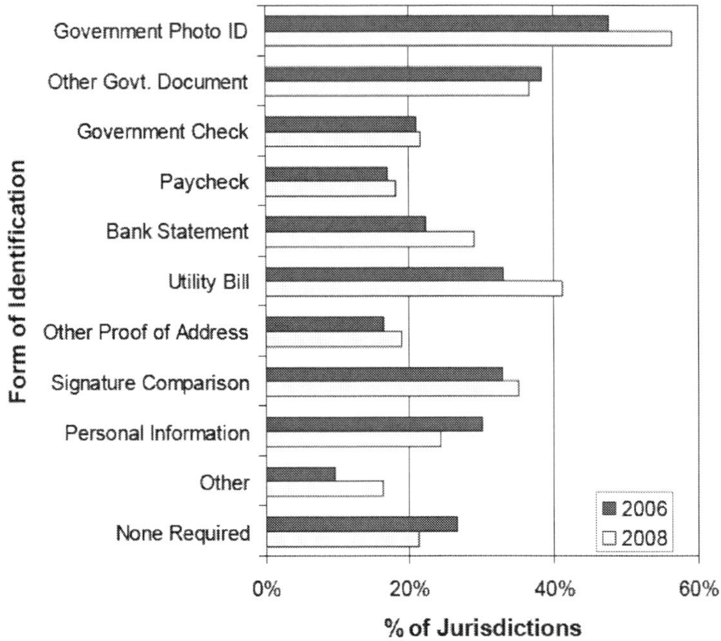

Source: Analysis by CRS of data from capstone surveys.

Notes: LEOs were asked to indicate all acceptable forms of identification. The option "Other Govt. Document" refers to those indicating the name and address of the voter, and "Personal Information" refers to address, date of birth, and so forth.

Figure 40. Percentage of Jurisdictions Requiring or Accepting Different Kinds of Identification for Voting, 2006 and 2008.

How often do non-eligible persons attempt to vote in your jurisdiction, either in person or by absentee ballot?65

- Do you agree or disagree that deliberate voter fraud is a serious problem in your jurisdiction?
- Do you believe that requiring photo identification of all voters would make elections more secure, less secure, or have no impact on election security?
- Do you believe that asking for photo identification of all voters would increase turnout, decrease turnout, or have no impact on turnout?

The results are presented in *Figure 41*. On average, LEOs mildly supported a requirement for photo identification. However, about 30% of respondents chose "extremely supportive," 5%-10% "do not support at all," and the choices of the other 60% were spread across the scale of possible responses. LEOs whose jurisdictions used hand-counted paper ballots were somewhat less supportive of photo ID than other jurisdictions, perhaps because those jurisdictions had many fewer voters on average than other jurisdictions (see *Figure 49* below), and those LEOs therefore might be more likely to know voters personally. DRE users, who tended to have large jurisdictions, were more supportive on average of photo ID than were users of other systems.

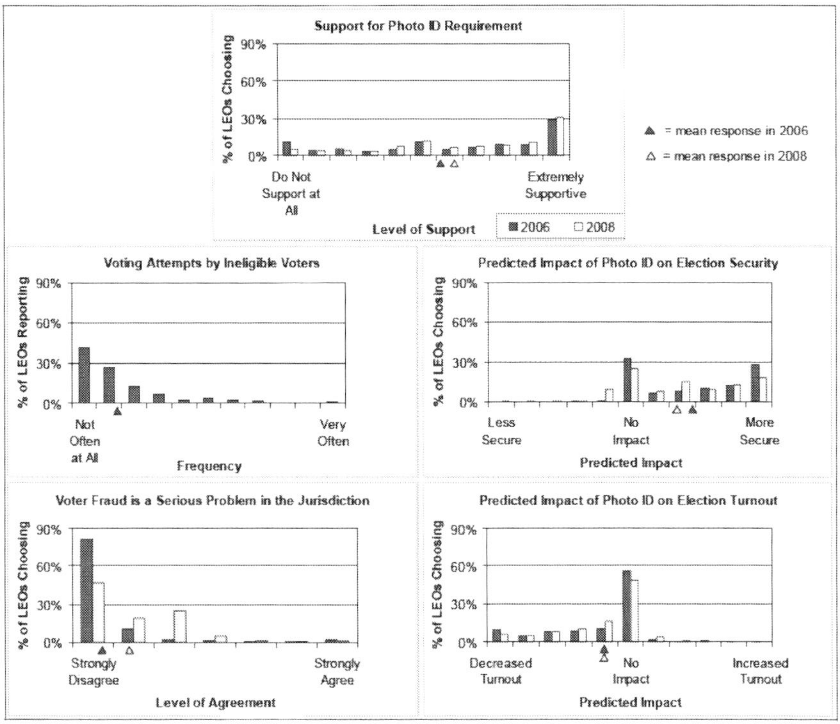

Source: Analysis by CRS of data from capstone surveys.

Figure 41. Frequency Distributions of Response by LEOs to Questions about Voter Identification, 2006 and 2008.

Two-thirds of LEOs also believed that requiring photo identification would make elections more secure. DRE users were more likely than users of other systems to believe that, but users of other systems did not differ significantly.

The support of LEOs for photo ID and their views about its impacts on security do not, however, appear to be based on concerns about ineligible voters or voter fraud, which few believed were problems in their jurisdictions. Furthermore, while about half of LEOs believed that requiring photo identification would have no impact on voter turnout, more than 40% believed that it would depress turnout.

Views did not change greatly from 2006 to 2008. LEOs were slightly more supportive of photo ID in 2008 and somewhat more concerned about fraud, but they were significantly less confident that photo ID would improve the security of elections.

The results appear to suggest an apparent discrepancy between, on the one hand, the overall support of LEOs for photo ID and their average views about its effects on security, and, on the other hand, their views about impacts on turnout and the risk of voter fraud—that is, they tended to support photo ID and believed it would increase security but at the same time they tended to believe that fraud was not a problem and that requiring photo ID would depress turnout. It is possible that however low the risk of fraud, LEOs believe reducing it outweighs any negative impact on turnout. Also, LEOs who supported photo ID were less likely than those who did not to believe that requiring photo ID would depress turnout, and they were more likely to believe that fraud was a problem and that photo ID would increase security. In any case, the range of perspectives in the responses to the questions shows that the controversy is not settled, even among local election officials.[66]

Election Administration Issues

Election Preparations

The Time that Leos Reported Spending Preparing for Elections Increased from 2004 to 2008

The 2006 election was the first under which all HAVA requirements were in effect.[67] Consistent with the perception of LEOs that HAVA has made elections more complex to administer (*Figure 33*), three-quarters found that they spent more time preparing for the 2006 than the 2004 election, and almost 90% reported spending more time in 2008 than 2006. For 2004 versus 2006, this perception was supported by comparing the number of hours per week LEOs reported spending on election duties. On average, the time spent increased 15%, from 21 to 24 hours.[68] This difference may be especially significant given that 2006 was not a presidential election year, during which additional work may be required than in intervening elections. However, the time spent did not change from 2006 to 2008—it was 24 hours in 2008 as well. There are several possible explanations for this discrepancy, and it was not possible to determine the cause.

Leos Believed that Better Voter Education Would Reduce Problems on Election Day and Improve the Overall Process

In 2008, LEOs were asked about voter education. About half reported that their jurisdictions had voter education programs intended to increase voters' knowledge of election rules and procedures. About 90% agreed that voter education about rules and procedures is important, and two-thirds that it is the responsibility of LEOs. About 60% believed that lack of voter knowledge creates problems in elections, and 80% that better voter education would improve the election-day process (*Figure 42*). Support was somewhat weaker for all those statements, although still positive on average, among LEOs whose jurisdictions did not have voter education programs.

The percentage of jurisdictions with voter-education programs varied with the kind of voting system (*Table 9*). Fewer than 20% of those using hand-counted paper ballots had such programs, whereas most using DREs did. Similarly, paper-ballot users indicated lower support than users of other systems for the statements in *Figure 42*, and they were neutral about whether educating voters is important or the responsibility of LEOs.

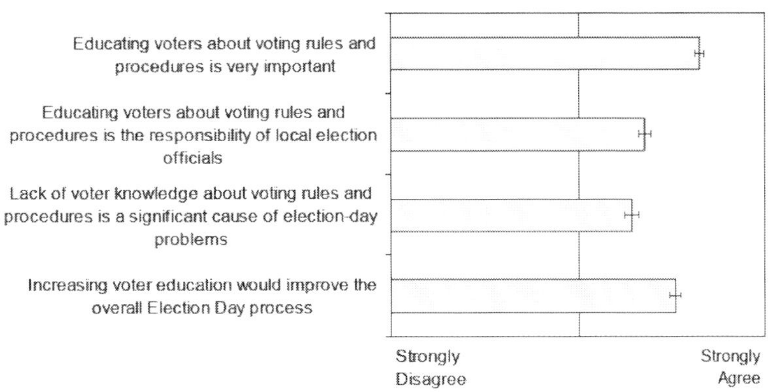

Source: Analysis by CRS of data from capstone surveys.

Notes: Data presented are mean responses on a scale of 1 to 7.

Figure 42. Agreement/Disagreement of LEOs with Statements About Voter Education, 2008.

Table 9. Percentage of Jurisdictions Using Different Kinds of Voting Systems That Reported Having a Voter-Education Program, 2008

Type of Voting System	%
Lever machine	53
Hand-counted paper ballots	18
Central-count optical scan (CCOS)	50
Precinct-count optical scan (PCOS)	41
Direct-recording electronic (DRE)	58

Source: Analysis by CRS of data from capstone surveys.

Incidents on Election Day

There have been several prominent issues of concern reported by the media in recent elections, such as voting-system malfunctions and problems with pollworkers, vendors, long lines, media coverage, and timely and accurate reporting of results. The surveys therefore presented a list of 16 potential problems and other events in 2006 and 2008 and asked LEOs to indicate which, if any, had occurred. The results are presented in *Table 10*. About 65% of survey respondents in 2006 and 50% in 2008 reported experiencing at least one of the events listed in the table. In 2006, more than 100 LEOs reported five or more kinds of incidents, with a maximum of 11, and in 2008, more than 50 experienced five or more, with a maximum of 10. Not surprisingly, LEOs in more populous jurisdictions reported more events than those in less populous ones. In 2008, about 1 in 15 LEOs reported an "uncontrollable" event such as a fire or a power outage.

In 2008 LEOs were asked to assess how successful the election process was in their jurisdictions. More than one-quarter reported a very successful process, and none considered it unsuccessful. However, the degree of success perceived was inversely related to the number of different types of incidents reported.

Given that 2008 was a presidential election, higher turnout was expected, and some variation in incidents might be related to whether a jurisdiction had higher turnout in 2008 than 2006. Seventy percent of LEOs reported higher turnout in 2008 (*Figure 43*), and LEOs in jurisdictions using hand-counted paper ballots reported a greater increase in turnout than those using other kinds of systems. However, those reporting higher turnout were not more likely to experience incidents.

The Most Commonly Reported Incident in the 2006 and 2008 Elections Was Malfunction of a DRE or Optical Scan System

About 65% of LEOs using DREs or PCOS as the primary voting system reported this problem. About 55% of CCOS users and about 40% of lever machine users reported this problem, with the lowest incidence, 20%, among LEOs using hand-counted paper ballots.[69] There was no significant difference between the surveys in the incidence of this problem.[70]

Table 10. Percentage of LEOs Reporting Various Events in Their Jurisdictions on Election Day, 2006 and 2008

	% o f LEOs Reporting	
Event	2006	2008
Repairable electronic voting system malfunction	60	59
Unrepairable electronic voting system malfunction	16	14
Electronic voting system was hacked	0	0
Vendors did not provide the support expected	18	6
Poll workers did not understand their jobs	30	34
Poll workers did not report for duty	14	13
Excessively long lines	16	15
Insufficient supply of paper ballots	5	4
Polling places failed to accurately report election results	3	2
Polling places failed to report election results in a timely manner	6	5
Central office failed to report election results in a timely manner	4	1
Unfair media coverage of election administration	15	7
A close race (2%-3% margin of victory)	32	31
A race resulting in an election recount	27	23
A race resulting in a legal challenge	3	6
Deliberate election fraud	1	2

Source: Analysis by CRS of data from capstone surveys.

Note: The percentages in this table are based on the total number of respondents who reported at least one kind of incident on election day (970 in 2006 and 670 in 2008). This base was chosen because it provided a reasonable basis of comparison among the kinds of incidents and between the surveys, given that the question did not have an option for LEOs to check if they had no problems whatever. Therefore, the percentages listed are likely to be overestimates of the actual percentage of jurisdictions that experienced the listed events. The percentages in the table would have been lower if the total number of LEOs responding to the survey had been used, but in that case the denominator would likely have included LEOs who experienced problems but skipped the question. An estimate relative to the total number of respondents can be calculated for each percentage in the table by multiplying the listed percentage by either 0.644 (2006 data) or 0.494 (2008 data).

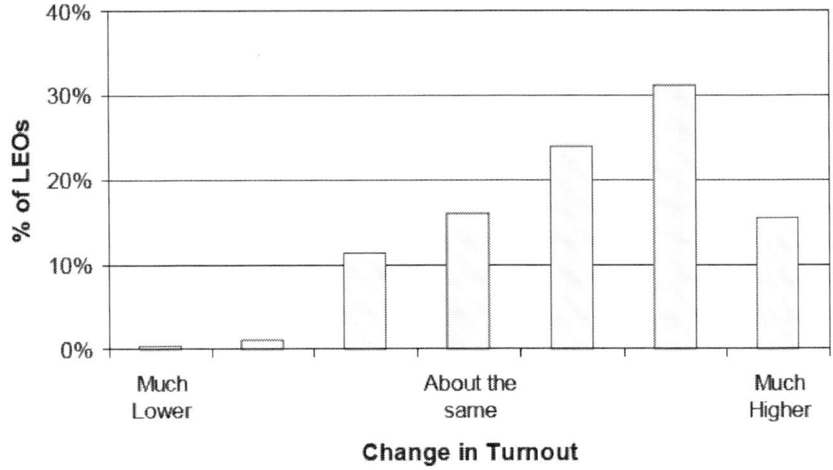

Source: Analysis by CRS of data from capstone surveys.

Figure 43. Assessment by LEOs of Whether Turnout Was Higher in 2008 Than 2006.

The reason for the low incidence among paper ballot users is not clear. It might be explained in part by the high proportion of those jurisdictions, about half, that used vote-by-phone to meet HAVA accessibility requirements (see *Figure 13* above).

While DRE users reported a slightly higher incidence of malfunction (67% of those reporting at least one event and about 50% of all DRE users) than PCOS users (63% of those reporting at least one event and about 48% of all users), a larger difference might have been expected. In jurisdictions where DREs are the primary voting system, several might be used in each polling place, whereas in PCOS jurisdictions, typically only one OS machine is used. Therefore, the chance of at least one malfunction would be expected to be higher on average in jurisdictions using DREs.[71] However, if DREs had lower failure rates per machine than optical scan systems, the difference would be correspondingly lower.[72]

The results suggest that current optical scan systems may not be significantly more reliable than DREs. They also contrast strikingly with the uniformly high ratings all users gave for the reliability of their voting systems (see *Figure 19* above).

LEOs did not appear to assess the malfunctions as being the result of tampering. In fact, only one reported a system being hacked, in 2006, and that was a precinct-count optical scan user.[73]

About 10% of LEOs were disappointed in the level of support provided by vendors. Those LEOs were more than twice as likely to have experienced malfunctions of their voting systems as LEOs who were not disappointed with vendor support.

Confusing Ballots Were Often a Problem

In 2008, ballots were slightly longer on average than they had been in 2004, but half of LEOs reported no difference. More than half reported that confusing ballots were a problem for voters in their jurisdictions in 2008 (*Figure 44*). About three-quarters believed that it would be beneficial to devote additional resources to ballot design. Not surprisingly, LEOs who were more concerned about ballot confusion were also more likely on average to believe that additional resources should be devoted to ballot design. About 40% of LEOs reported that they had little or no familiarity with ballot-design studies and best practices, about half were moderately familiar, and only about 10% reported a high level of familiarity.

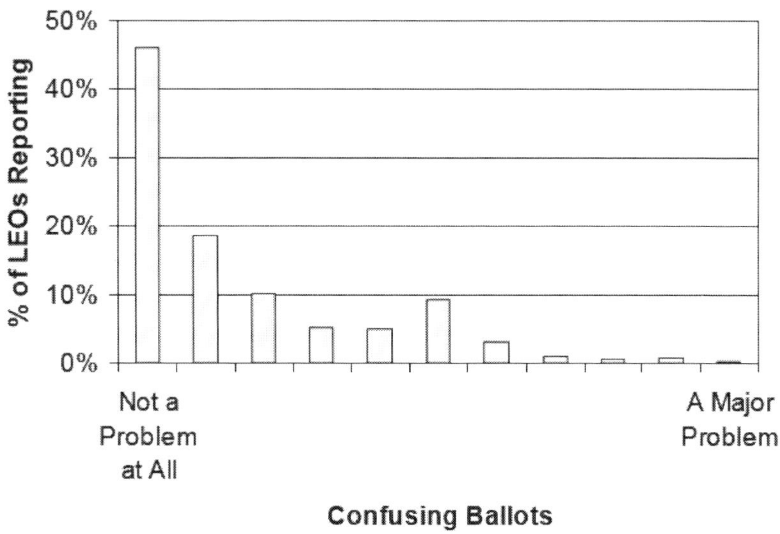

Source: Analysis by CRS of data from capstone surveys.

Figure 44. Assessment by LEOs of Whether Confusing Ballots Were a Problem for Voters, 2008.

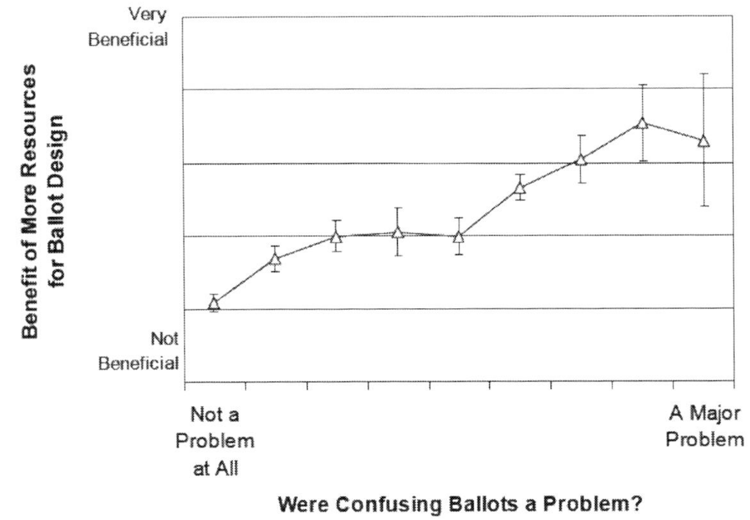

Source: Analysis by CRS of data from capstone surveys.

Notes: The graph shows mean responses on benefit of LEOs choosing different ratings for whether ballots were confusing. Ratings of 8 to 10 (on a scale of 0 to 10) for the latter were combined because of small sample sizes.

Figure 45. Relationship Between Assessments by LEOs About Confusing Ballots and Whether Additional Resources for Ballot Design Would Be Useful, 2008.

The Incidence of Long Lines at the Polling Place Was Highest in Jurisdictions Using Dres

Another notable result was the fairly high incidence of LEOs who reported excessively long lines at the polling place. About 11% of all respondents reported long lines in 2006, and 7% in 2008. The prevalence was much higher in jurisdictions using DREs primarily, occurring in about one quarter in 2006 and 14% in 2008. In those using other kinds of voting systems, long lines were reported by only about 5% of respondents in both surveys. Jurisdictions using DREs also reported more unfair media coverage (19% in 2006 and 7% in 2008) than users of other systems (5% in 2006 and 2% in 2008).

The incidence of problems with accurate and timely reporting of election results was low. It did not differ among users of the different kinds of voting systems, except for lever machine users. They reported a much higher incidence, about 10%, of failure of polling places to report accurately in both surveys. That was about five times the rate of users of other voting systems.

Reports of deliberate election fraud of any kind were also few—8 LEOs in 2006 and 14 in 2008, under 1% of jurisdictions. Such a rate might nevertheless be considered unacceptably high, depending on such factors as the seriousness of the offense, the impact on the election of such attempts at fraud, and the degree to which election officials are able to detect all such attempts.

In 2006, the number of elections requiring recounts that LEOs reported was much higher (264, which was 18% of all survey respondents and 27% of LEOs reporting incidents) than in 2008 (156, 12% of respondents and 23% of those reporting incidents). Not surprisingly, recounts were much more likely to be reported when a race was close. They were also more likely in jurisdictions using lever machines and hand-counted paper ballots than optical scan or DRE systems.

LEOs noticed no change on average in residual votes (overvotes plus undervotes plus spoiled ballots) from 2004 to 2006.[74] About 60% reported no change, and about 20% each reported an increase or a decrease. This result suggests that the decreased confidence LEOs had in 2006 in the ability of voting systems to reduce voter error was not a result of a noticeable increase in such error. Alternatively, the decrease in confidence might have resulted from sources such as changes in media coverage of voting-system problems.

The number of provisional ballots used varied greatly among jurisdictions in 2006. About 30% of that variability was explainable by the number of voters in the jurisdiction. Thus, jurisdictions with fewer than 1,000 registered voters used about 10 provisional ballots on average and those with more than 100,000 voters used 1,500. Across all jurisdictions, one provisional ballot was used for every 140 registered voters on average.[75] About a quarter of jurisdictions, mostly small, used no provisional ballots, and about 4% used more than 1,000, with a maximum of 15,000 reported by a jurisdiction with about half a million voters.

In 2008, LEOs were asked for the percentage of ballots cast that were provisional, rather than the number cast. About one-third used no provisional ballots. In about half of jurisdictions, some were cast but accounted for 1% or fewer of all ballots. In about 15%, they accounted for 1%-5% of all ballots, and in about 6% of jurisdictions, they accounted for more than 5%. About 2% of jurisdictions stated that at least one polling place had run out of provisional ballots during the election. The percentage of provisional ballots cast did not vary with the size of the jurisdiction. Also, 36% of LEOs reported an increase in the use of provisional ballots in comparison to 2006, while 26% reported a decrease.

When asked whether provisional ballots were easier to use than they had been in the previous election, LEOs found them slightly easier to use on average in 2006 and again in 2008. However, there was far more variability in the 2008 results, with higher proportions of LEOs finding them both easier and more difficult than in the previous election (**Table 11**). The reasons for the increased variation are not clear.

Table 11. Assessments of LEOs About Whether Provisional Ballots Were Easier or More Difficult to Use Than in the Previous Election, 2006 and 2008

Change from Previous Election	2006	2008
Easier	16%	36%
The Same	75%	38%
More Difficult	9%	26%

Source: Analysis by CRS of data from capstone surveys.

The Percentage of Jurisdictions Offering Early Voting Increased Substantially from 2006 to 2008

The percentage of jurisdictions offering early voting increased from about half in 2006 to nearly two-thirds in 2008, and most LEOs reported that the number of early voters increased in 2008. In 2006, about a third each of jurisdictions offering early voting reported using optical scan, a third DREs, and fewer than one in ten paper ballots. In 2008, more than half used optical scan, with about a third offering CCOS and a quarter PCOS, while almost half used DREs and about one in six paper ballots.[76] In 2008, a quarter of jurisdictions used two different kinds of voting systems for early voting, and a few offered three. Among those using more than one system, only about 10% did not use DREs. About half used CCOS and DREs, a quarter PCOS and DREs, and a fifth paper ballots and DREs. In 2008, a higher proportion of votes were cast early in jurisdictions using DREs as their main voting system (27%) than in those using other systems (14%) (see *Figure 46*).

The rate of absentee voting has been increasing nationally over the last several elections, as the number of states offering early and "no excuse" absentee voting has increased.[77] In both 2006 and 2008, 85%-90% of jurisdictions used only one kind of voting system for absentee ballots, with most of the rest using two, and a few three. About three-quarters of jurisdictions used optical scan systems, and about one-quarter used paper ballots. About 10% reported using DREs. In most cases these were for "in-person absentee ballots,"[78] but in some cases, LEOs reported that election officials entered choices submitted on paper ballots into DREs.

The survey asked LEOs to provide information on the percentage of all votes cast by absentee voting in 2006 and 2008. The average reported was about 15% in each election, with 1%-5% being most common in both elections (*Figure 47*). However, most LEOs reported that the number of absentee ballots increased in 2008.[79] In contrast to early voting, CCOS jurisdictions had a higher proportion of ballots cast via absentee (26%) than did jurisdictions using other systems (13%) (*Figure 46*). The overall average rate is very similar to the ones reported in the EAC's election day surveys (14.2% for 2006 and 17.3% for 2008).[80]

Most Leos Received Voted Ballots from Military and Overseas Voters after the Deadline

In 2008, more than 95% of LEOs reported receiving requests for ballots from military and overseas voters. However, 62% also reported receiving voted ballots[81] from such voters after the deadline for receiving ballots. Many LEOs provided suggestions for ways to improve participation by such voters, which varies by state. The most common by far was to permit greater use of electronic methods—fax, e-mail, and Internet. Other common suggestions were more time for preparing, distributing, and processing ballots for such voters, improved training and awareness of voters and military personnel, and ways of improving the currency of address information.

Some observers have expressed concerns about early and "no excuse" absentee voting, arguing, among other things, that they do not increase turnout and that they pose some security risks. These concerns were largely not shared by LEOs (*Figure 48*). About three-quarters agreed that absentee voting should be considered a voter's right, and about half that early voting should be.[82] Most also agreed that absentee voting is worth the costs, and that verification of authenticity is not difficult for those ballots.

LEOs were equivocal about whether early voting was worth the costs in 2006 but supported it on average in 2008. Among users of different kinds of voting systems, lever-machine users were somewhat negative, DRE users were positive, and those using paper ballots and optical scan were neutral. All except lever-machine users believed on average that early voting should be a right, and users of all systems believed that absentee voting should be a right.

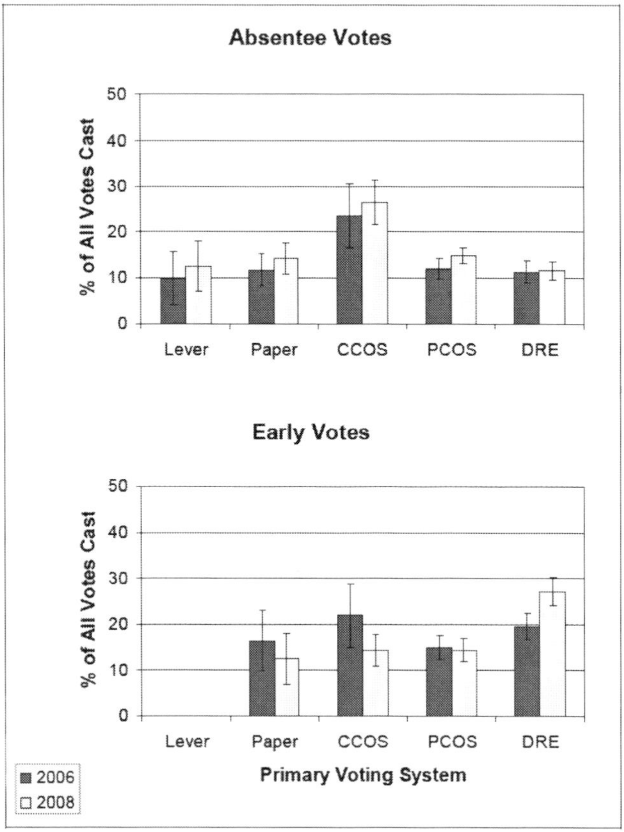

Source: Analysis by CRS of data from capstone surveys.

Notes: Data presented are means for jurisdictions using each type of voting system. Early voting data for lever machine jurisdictions are excluded because too few reported using early voting to provide meaningful results for the chart.

Figure 46. Mean Percentage of Ballots Cast via Absentee and Early Voting as a Function of Primary Voting System Type in a Jurisdiction, 2006 and 2008.

Problems with Pollworkers Were Common

About 10% of jurisdictions experienced one or more instances of pollworkers not reporting for duty (see *Table 10* above). Since the average jurisdiction used more than 150 pollworkers, the impact may be small on average (although not necessarily in the affected polling places). Nevertheless, absenteeism among pollworkers has been cited as a significant problem on election day.[83] Factors that might contribute include long hours, low pay, poor training, and age or illness, but analysis of pay and training data from the survey did not point to those factors as being significant.[84]

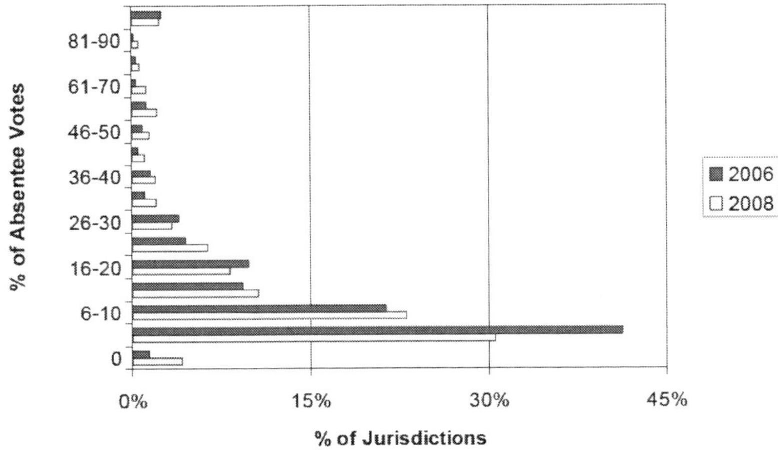

Source: Analysis by CRS of data from capstone surveys.

Figure 47. Percentage of Votes LEOs Reported as Cast via Absentee Voting, 2006 and 2008.

About 20% of LEOs reported instances of pollworkers who did not understand their jobs.[85] The lowest rate was in jurisdictions using hand-counted paper ballots. Results from LEOs using other kinds of voting systems were substantially higher, but did not differ significantly from one another. It seems unlikely that the differences between the results for paper and those for other voting systems arose purely from differences in the roles of technology in the different voting systems, since the technology-related tasks of pollworkers in jurisdictions using CCOS are unlikely to be much greater than those in jurisdictions using paper ballots. There are several other possible factors. For example, the average total number of pollworkers, polling places, and registered voters reported by LEOs is far lower for jurisdictions using paper ballots than for any other voting system (see *Figure 49* in the next section). Also, the quality of training and the background and experience of pollworkers are likely to vary among jurisdictions.

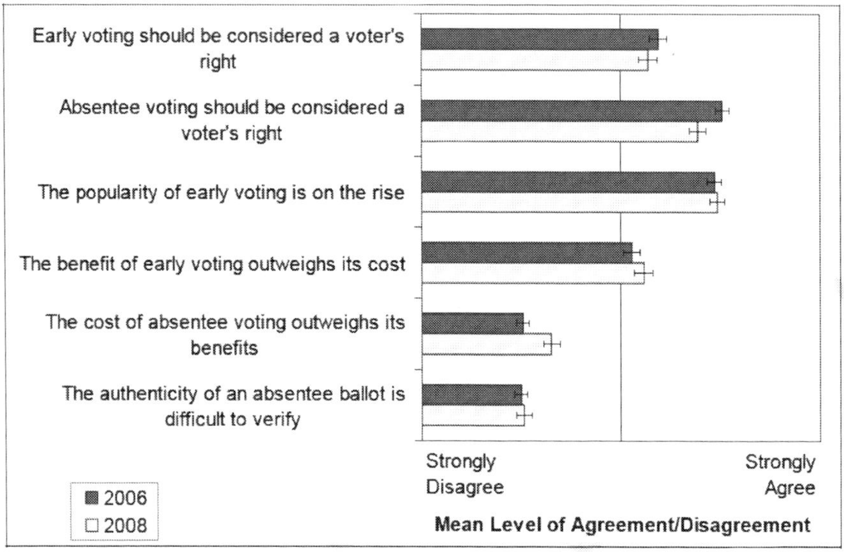

Source: Analysis by CRS of data from capstone surveys.

Figure 48. Agreement/Disagreement by LEOs with Statements About Absentee and Early Voting, 2006 and 2008.

Use, Training, and Experience of Pollworkers

The 2006 and 2008 surveys included several additional questions about pollworkers. More than 95% of LEOs reported using one or more pollworkers, with a mean number of more than 200 in a jurisdiction[86] and a maximum of more than 10,000. The number of pollworkers in the jurisdictions was strongly correlated with the number of registered voters reported, as was the total number of polling places. The kind of voting system used also varied with the number of registered voters.

Overall, jurisdictions using hand-counted paper ballots had the smallest number of registered voters, polling places, and pollworkers, and those using DREs and lever machines the highest (*Figure 49*). On average, there were 5-10 pollworkers per polling place. Jurisdictions using lever machines and DREs had the lowest number, and those using other voting systems did not differ significantly from each other. There were about 1,000 voters per polling place on average, with jurisdictions using paper ballots having the fewest, about 600. The pattern was similar for the number of registered voters per pollworker, with an overall average of 160, and 100 for paper-ballot jurisdictions.[87]

While *Figure 49* suggests that the number of registered voters, polling places, and pollworkers increased in 2008, the large variation among jurisdictions meant that the only statistically significant increase was for pollworkers per polling place, which increased slightly for PCOS jurisdictions.

Compensation of pollworkers also varied substantially. Respondents reported paying pollworkers $100 on average for work on election day.[88] The results suggest that there is significant variation among the states, with averages ranging from a low of about $30 to a high of more than $200. Very few respondents reported paying nothing to pollworkers. Rates of pay did not vary significantly with the number of registered voters or type of voting system used, and it did not change significantly from 2006 to 2008.

Pay also did not vary with performance. LEOs who reported problems with pollworker performance paid them no less per day on average than those who did not. However, the survey did not explore potentially influential demographic factors such as age of pollworkers or average cost of living.

Perhaps more surprisingly, the amount of training pollworkers received was also not associated statistically with reports of performance problems, in either survey.[89] However, more LEOs than not believed that inadequate training was responsible for problems with election administration (*Figure 50*), with DRE users expressing the most concern and paper-ballot users the least. Most also believed that training needs significant improvement (*Figure 51*), with lever machine and DRE users expressing the most concern and paper-ballot users the least. The overall level of concern about the impact of inadequate training and the need to improve it was somewhat lower in 2008 than 2006. Not surprisingly, in both surveys LEOs who believed more strongly that inadequate training caused problems also tended to believe more strongly that improvements in training were needed.

In both surveys, 93% of LEOs reported that pollworkers received training, about two to three hours on average (*Figure 52*).[90] Seventy percent of LEOs considered pollworker training "extremely important," and only a few considered it "not important at all."[91] The amount of training was about 20% lower on average for jurisdictions using paper ballots than other kinds of voting systems. In just under 10% of jurisdictions, training was 1 hour or less. In three quarters, it was 2-4 hours, and in only 5% was it one day or more.

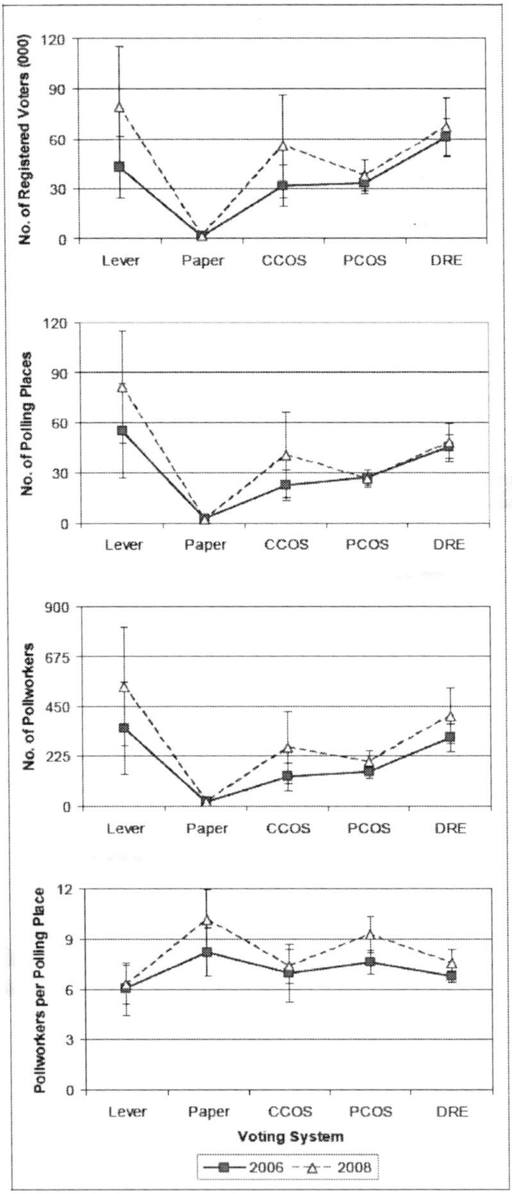

Source: Analysis by CRS of data from capstone surveys.

Note: See note for Figure 11 for an explanation of types of voting systems, and note for Figure 15.

Figure 49. Relationships Between Kinds of Voting Systems Used and Selected Characteristics of Jurisdictions, 2006 and 2008.

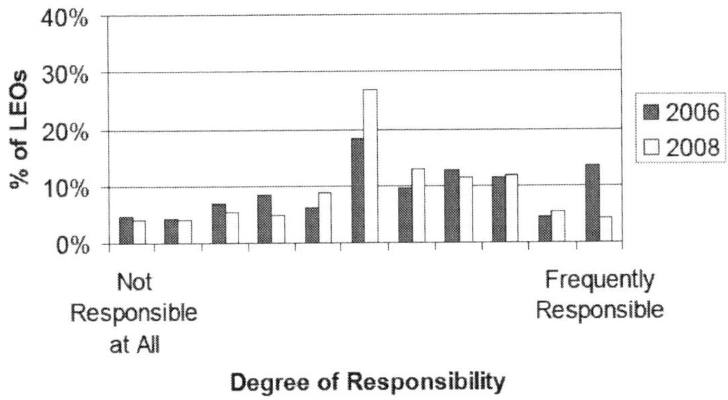

Source: Analysis by CRS of data from capstone surveys.

Figure 50. Views of LEOs on the Responsibility of Inadequate Pollworker Training for Problems with Election Administration, 2006 and 2008.

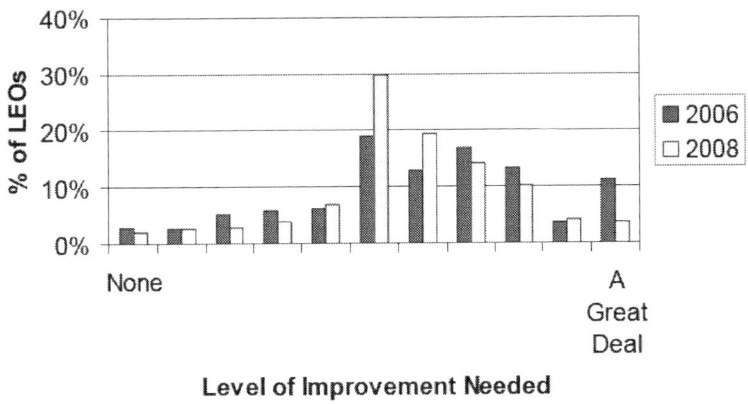

Source: Analysis by CRS of data from capstone surveys.

Figure 51. Views of LEOs on the Need for Improvement of Pollworker Training, 2006 and 2008.

In 2008, LEOs were asked their views about the best method for training pollworkers. Nine out of 10 believed that classroom training was most effective, with the rest preferring reading materials, Internet, or other methods, such as instruction at the polling place.

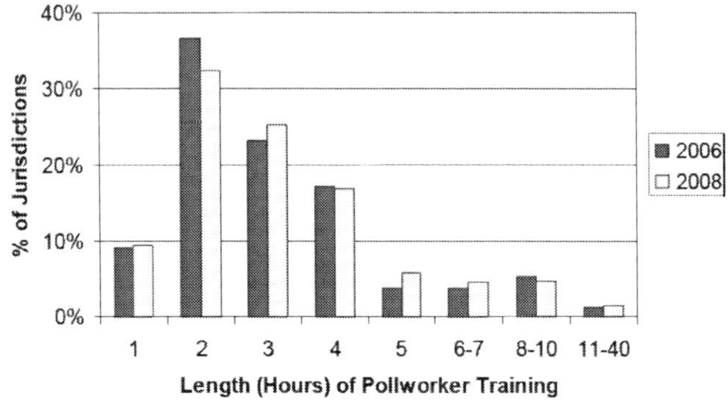

Source: Analysis by CRS of data from capstone surveys.

Figure 52. Number of Hours of Pollworker Training Reported by LEOs, 2006 and 2008.

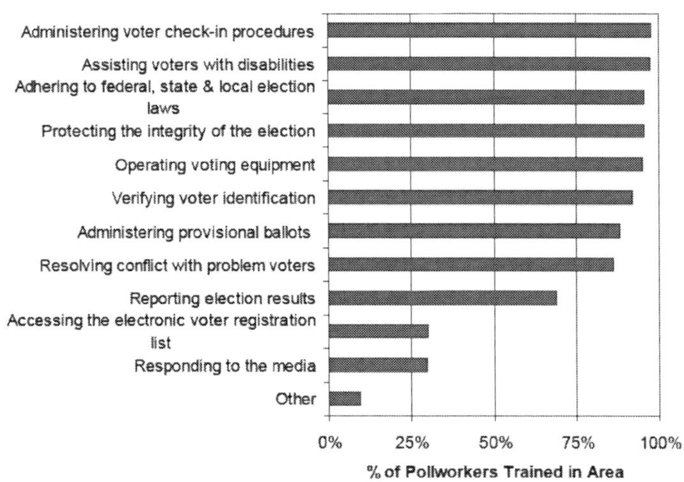

Source: Analysis by CRS of data from capstone surveys.

Figure 53. Areas of Training for Pollworkers Reported by LEOs, 2006.

There appeared to be substantial uniformity among jurisdictions in the areas in which pollworkers were trained (*Figure 53*),[92] with more than 90% being trained in voter check-in, accessibility, election laws, operation of voting machines, and election integrity. LEOs were not asked what areas of training should be improved, but another study that surveyed pollworkers in New Mexico found that many desired more training in voting-machine operation and election laws.[93] Interestingly, that finding reflects the views of many LEOs about their own training, as discussed earlier in this report.

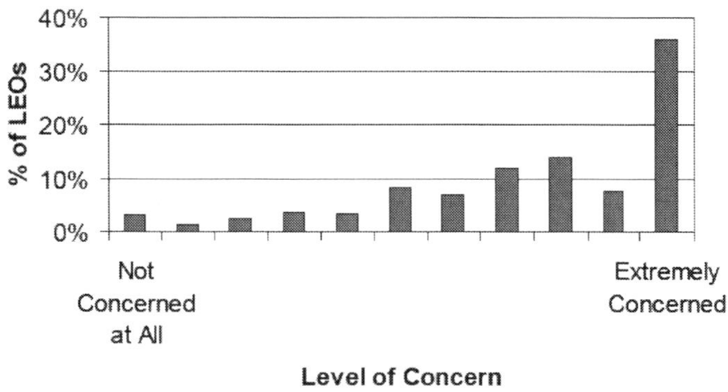

Source: Analysis by CRS of data from capstone surveys.

Figure 54. Level of Concern Reported by LEOs About the Negative Impact of Increased Election Complexity on Pollworker Recruitment, 2006.

LEOs also believed that HAVA is changing the nature of pollworker training, with 20% reporting that the changes were "substantial." As reported earlier (see *Table 6 and Figure 33* above), most LEOs believed that HAVA has made elections more complex to administer. In 2006, most also expressed concern that the increased complexity of elections would have a negative impact on recruitment of pollworkers, and more than a third of respondents were "extremely concerned" (*Figure 54*).[94] In 2008, most agreed with the statement that recruiting pollworkers was difficult, but nevertheless felt equally strongly that the number of pollworkers in their jurisdictions was adequate, and that the pollworkers had the necessary knowledge and skills to perform effectively. LEOs were also neutral about whether the increased technological complexity of voting systems has made it difficult for pollworkers to perform their election-day duties (*Figure 55*).

Users of hand-counted paper-ballot systems expressed the most positive views about their pollworkers. They felt most strongly that the number of pollworkers they had was adequate, and they were the only set of users who were neutral about the difficulty of recruiting pollworkers. DRE users might have been expected to have the highest concerns about pollworker knowledge and skills, but in fact lever-machine users expressed the most concern.

HAVA established two programs to provide incentives for student participation in election administration, one for high school and the other for college students.[95] To help identify what impacts those programs might have had, LEOs were asked in 2008 whether they had experienced an increase in high-school and college student volunteers. About one-quarter reported an increase (*Figure 55*), but it could not be determined for this report which respondents were in jurisdictions that may have benefited from those programs. However, DRE users were the most likely to report an increase, and lever-machine and paper-ballot users the least likely.

Nonpartisan Election Officials

Some observers have suggested that the environment in which election officials operate is too politically contentious and that steps should be taken to make election administration more nonpartisan. For example, some believe that state election officials should not be permitted to be involved in political campaigns other than for their own positions. The 2006 and 2008 surveys asked LEOs several questions about this issue. In general, LEOs were satisfied with election administration at the state level (*Figure 56*), with only about 10% expressing significant dissatisfaction. More LEOs than not also believed that election administration in their state was independent of partisan politics.[96] Those views did not change significantly from 2006 to 2008 and they did not vary depending on whether a LEO was elected or appointed.

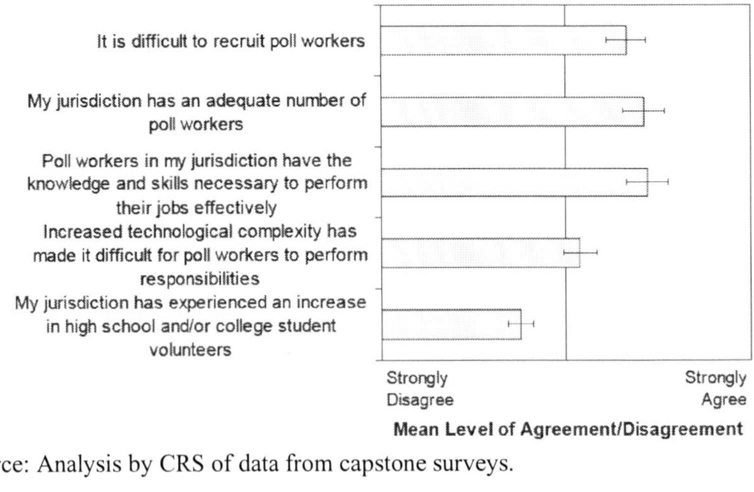

Source: Analysis by CRS of data from capstone surveys.

Figure 55. Agreement/Disagreement of LEOs with Statements About Pollworkers, 2008.

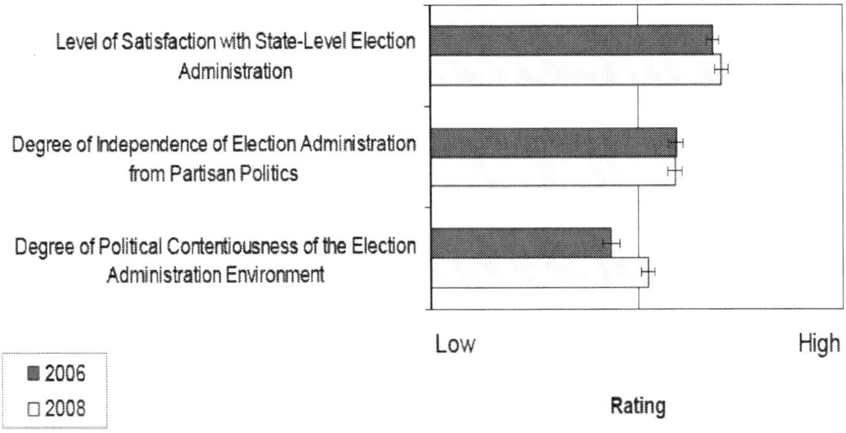

Source: Analysis by CRS of data from capstone surveys.

Figure 56. Assessments by LEOs About Aspects of the Election Administration Environment, 2006 and 2008.

In 2008, LEOs were asked whether the state role in local elections had changed in the last five years. Not surprisingly, three-quarters believed the state role had increased. About 60% of those who believed the state role had changed considered the effects of that change beneficial in their jurisdictions.

There was more variation in the views of LEOs about the political contentiousness of the election-administration environment, with more believing it contentious in 2008 than 2006. LEOs who were appointed were more likely to find the environment contentious than those who were elected, although that difference was not significant in 2008. In 2008, LEOs were asked if the degree of contention had increased since the last election. While more than half believed there had been no change, a greater percentage believed it had increased than that it had decreased. About 40% believed that the political environment had made election administration more difficult, while half believed it had made no difference.

In 2006, LEOs were also asked whether election administration should be a civil service function in their state. About half had no opinion, but significantly more elected LEOs were opposed to the idea than favored it. Appointed LEOs were evenly divided (*Figure 57*).

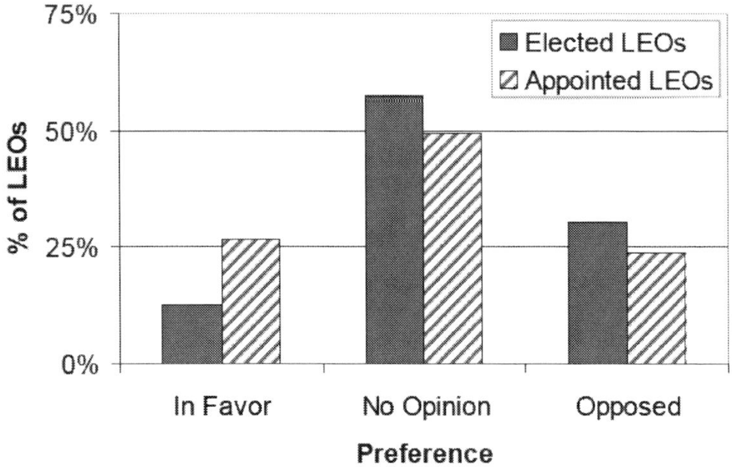

Source: Analysis by CRS of data from capstone surveys.

Figure 57. Views of LEOs About Whether Election Administration Should Be Part of the Civil Service in Their States, 2006.

POSSIBLE CAVEATS

As with all surveys, care needs to be taken in drawing inferences from the results. One question that could arise is whether the sample is representative of LEOs as a whole. For example, simply drawing the sample at random from the nationwide pool of election administrators would have resulted in a disproportionately large number of jurisdictions from New England and the upper Midwest, where elections are administered by townships rather than counties.[97] Steps were taken in the design of the studies to minimize the risk that the sample would not be representative (see the *Appendix* below). Overall, neither the sample design nor the characteristics of the responses suggest that the results are unrepresentative of the views and characteristics of local election officials.

Another potential caution for interpretation relates to the inherent limits of surveys such as these. In particular, there is no way to guarantee that the responses of the election officials correspond to their actual beliefs. In addition, there is no way to be certain that any particular belief corresponds to reality. The question on voting-system characteristics (see *Figure 19*) provides an illustration of the possibility for disparity. For several reasons, LEOs might be reluctant to rate their voting systems low in reliability, accuracy, and security, despite the anonymity of the results. Alternatively, they might truly believe that their voting systems are highly reliable, accurate, and secure, even if independent evidence does not support that view.

Also, some caution is needed in assigning cause and effect. The mere existence of an association or correlation between a factor and an effect does not necessarily mean that the factor caused the effect. For example, the survey showed a strong association between the kind of voting system used in a jurisdiction and the number of pollworkers (see *Figure 49*). However, while the kind of voting system may have some independent effect, a more important factor is likely to be the number of registered voters.

A final caution involves how survey results might be used to inform policy decisions. On the one hand, the results could be used to support the shaping of policy in directions expressed by LEOs in their responses. In many cases, such policy changes might be appropriate. On the other hand, it is possible that at least some of those desired changes would not in fact yield the most effective or appropriate policies. In such cases, the results might more constructively be used to help policymakers identify issues for which improvements in communication and understanding are needed.

POTENTIAL POLICY IMPLICATIONS

The survey results may have policy implications for several issues at the federal, state, and local levels of government. Some issues that may be relevant for congressional deliberations are highlighted below.

Election Officials

Many observers have commented favorably on the experience and dedication of the nation's local election officials. Survey results are consistent with that view. At the same time, other observers, including some election officials, have called for increased professionalism in election administration. Some survey results suggest areas of potential professional improvement, such as in education and in professional involvement at the national level. Congress could address this potential need by several means, for example facilitating educational and training programs for LEOs and promoting professional certification of election officials by entities accredited through the EAC or a professional association.

The seemingly unique demographic characteristics of LEOs as a group of government officials may have other policy implications, but they are not altogether clear. However, some observers may argue that efforts should be undertaken to ensure that LEOs reflect the diversity of the workforce or voting population as a whole, especially with respect to minority representation.

The issue of partisanship among election officials has been controversial for several years. Most national attention has been on state officials, but, given that most LEOs are elected and only about half the local jurisdictions in the United States are administered on a nonpartisan or bipartisan basis, policymakers may wish to consider the influence of partisanship among LEOs.

Voting Systems

Since the enactment of HAVA, controversy has arisen over whether DRE voting systems are sufficiently secure and reliable. The survey revealed that LEOs who have experience with DREs are very confident in them, consider them superior for accessibility, and do not generally support the addition of a voter-verified paper audit trail (VVPAT) to address security concerns, although those who use a VVPAT are satisfied with its performance. However, LEOs using other systems are much less confident in DREs and more supportive of VVPAT. The strongly dichotomous results suggest that as Congress considers whether to require changes in the security mechanisms used in voting systems, it might be useful to determine whether DRE users are overconfident in the security of their systems and procedures in practice, or, alternatively, whether nonusers might be misinformed about the reliability and security of DRE systems.[98]

The Help America Vote Act (HAVA)

The survey results suggest that HAVA is in the process of achieving several of its policy goals. The general and increasing support of most HAVA provisions—including those such as the creation of the EAC and the provisional ballot requirement that have been somewhat controversial—implies that most LEOs are in agreement with the goals of the act and are active partners in its implementation.

The overwhelming selection by jurisdictions of new voting systems that assist voters in avoiding errors indicates that the HAVA goal of reducing avoidable voter error is in the process of being met. The areas of concern expressed by LEOs—such as how to meet the costs of ongoing implementation of HAVA requirements—raise issues that Congress may wish to address as it considers HAVA appropriations and reauthorization.

The close relationship between LEOs and the vendors of their voting systems seems unlikely to change as a result of HAVA. However, with the codification by HAVA of the voting system standards and certification processes, the influence of the federal government in decisions about new voting systems might be expected to increase in relation to that of vendors and others. The increased concerns of LEOs in 2006 that vendors, media, political parties, and advocacy groups have too much influence on such decisions may bear consideration.

Research Needs

Scientific opinion surveys of local election officials are rare,[99] and additional research may be useful to address some of the matters raised by these studies. For example, a survey of state election officials might provide useful information and might additionally be helpful in assessing the most appropriate federal role in promoting the effective implementation of HAVA goals at all levels of government.

One common suggestion of LEOs for improving HAVA was to provide a means of adjusting requirements to fit the needs of smaller jurisdictions. To determine what, if any, such adjustments would be appropriate, it may be useful to have specific information on how the needs and characteristics of different jurisdictions vary with size—something that was beyond the scope of these surveys. It could also be useful to identify how the duties of LEOs vary with size and other characteristics of the jurisdiction. In many jurisdictions, election administration is only part of the LEO's job. It is not known to what degree these other responsibilities might affect election administration—negatively or positively.

Finally, these surveys have provided only snapshots of LEO characteristics and perceptions over three election cycles. It might be beneficial to perform similar surveys periodically to identify trends and explore new questions and issues.

Appendix. Notes on Methodology

The results presented and analyzed in this report are from three surveys sponsored by CRS as part of its Capstone program and performed by graduate students and faculty at the George Bush School of Government and Public Service at Texas A&M University in 2004 and 2006, and the Department of Political Science at the University of Oklahoma in 2008.[100] For both studies the CRS project manager was Eric Fischer and the project liaison was Kevin Coleman.[101]

The topics for the surveys were developed collaboratively by CRS and Texas A&M and University of Oklahoma participants. The major factor in choosing the topics was potential usefulness of the results for Congress. The Bush School and University of Oklahoma teams developed and administered the survey instruments in consultation with CRS and provided the authors with the data used in performing the analyses.

The three surveys were conducted after the November 2004, 2006, and 2008 federal elections, between December and the following April. For each survey, a sample of approximately 3,800 LEOs was drawn from the roughly 9,000 election jurisdictions in the 50 states.[102] To ensure that LEOs from all states were included, but that states with large numbers of LEOs were not disproportionately represented (see *Figure A-1*), a modified random-sampling regime was used, as follows: Surveys were sent to all LEOs in states with 150 or fewer local jurisdictions. For the ten states with more than 150 LEOs, a sample of 150 was chosen at random from the local jurisdictions, and surveys were sent to those LEOs.[103]

Each survey was initially distributed in the month following the election (December). Administration was mostly electronic, with respondents visiting a website to enter their responses. In cases where electronic administration was not possible, LEOs were sent paper surveys via the U.S. Postal Service. Those who did not respond were sent reminders or contacted by telephone, with the survey response period closing in March or April following the election.

For each survey, the overall final response rate was about 40% of the sample, or about 17% of all jurisdictions in the United States. Respondents answered 85%-90% of questions, on average.[104] The response was sufficiently high to permit statistical analysis and comparison of the results among the surveys. The distribution of responses among states was similar across the surveys (see *Figure A-2*). Individual response rates per state were between

25% and 50% for about three-quarters of states. The remainder were evenly split between those for which under 25% of LEOs responded, and those for which the rate was greater than 50%. Response rates did not vary significantly for any survey with the number of local election jurisdictions in a state or its voting age population. About 70% of respondents worked in county election jurisdictions, with most of the remainder working in townships (*Figure A-3*). The small difference among the surveys in those choosing "town/township" and in those choosing "other" was almost certainly a result of a small change in the structure of the question after the 2004 survey.[105] However, as the figure implies, the proportion of respondents from county jurisdictions increased slightly over the course of the three surveys.

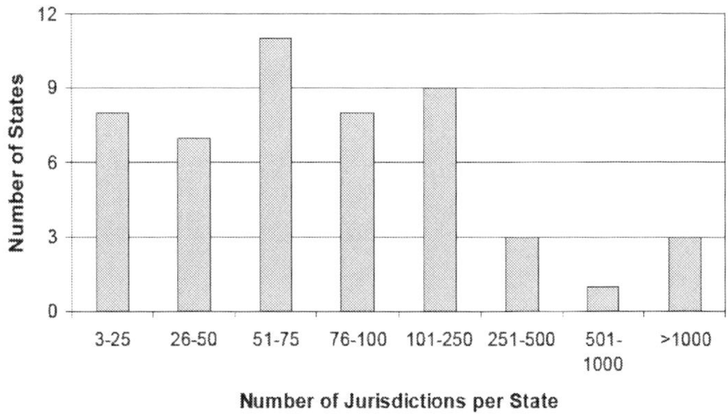

Source: CRS analysis of data provided by the Election Reform Information Project (electionline.org) and other sources.

Note: Data are from 2004, but the distribution of jurisdictions did not change significantly across the surveys.

Figure A-1. Frequency Distribution of the Number of Local Election Jurisdictions in the States, 2004.

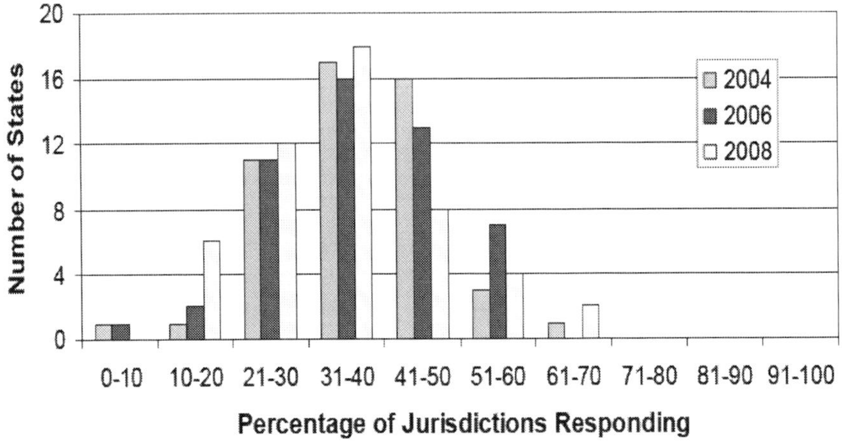

Source: Analysis by CRS of data from capstone surveys.

Figure A-2. Frequency Distribution of Response Rates by State.

All the results presented in this report are from analyses by CRS of data provided from the surveys by researchers at Texas A&M University (2004 and 2006) and the University of Oklahoma (2008). The raw data were first examined for errors, and corrections were made where necessary, in a few cases, such as if a LEO claimed to work more hours per week than is physically possible.[106] Where the correct answer could be reasonably discerned, the response was corrected.[107] Otherwise it was discarded. Once cleaned, the data were analyzed using standard parametric methods, mainly analysis of variance, linear regression, and Student's t-tests as appropriate.

Three kinds of hypotheses were tested:

- differences between groups, such as whether results differed across the three surveys;
- differences from a hypothetical value, such as whether LEOs were neutral about, agreed with, or disagreed with a particular statement; and
- tests for associations, such as whether the number of pollworkers in a jurisdiction was correlated with the number of registered voters.

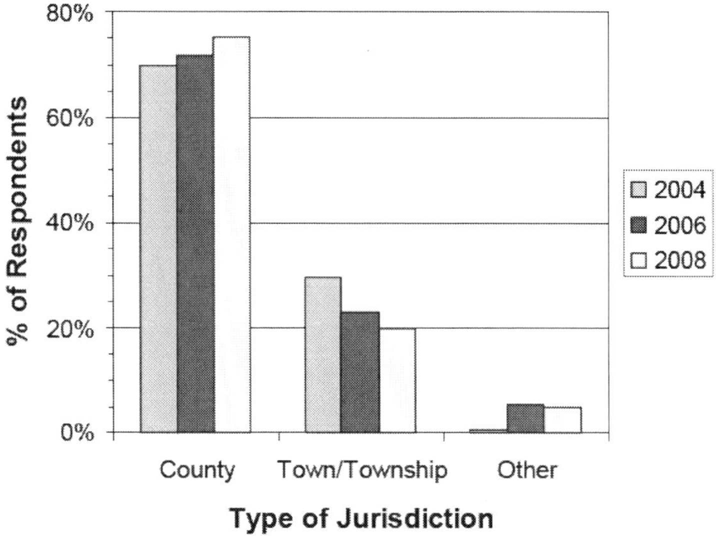

Source: Analysis by CRS of data from capstone surveys.

Note: In each survey, the choices for kind of jurisdiction were county, town, township, borough, and other. For this graph, the replies for town and township were combined, as were the replies for borough and other.

Figure A-3. Kinds of Jurisdictions Administered by Survey Respondents.

Statistical significance was determined using a significance level (α) of .01. However, for display purposes, graphs with error bars were drawn showing 95% confidence intervals for the means.

Most tests for which results are presented in this report yielded highly statistically significant results—p-values much lower than the significance level (p << .01). For reported data where statistically significant effects were not found, the lack of effect is noted in the text, for example, by stating that no change was found between 2004 and 2006 for a particular survey item.

ACKNOWLEDGMENTS

Many people provided helpful assistance in the development of this report. The authors wish to thank the following in particular for their invaluable contributions:

The principal investigators at Texas A&M University and the University of Oklahoma were Drs. Donald P. Moynihan and Carol L. Silva for the 2004 survey, and Carol L. Silva for 2006 and 2008. Ten graduate students participated in the first survey: Jennifer Gray, Marshall Gray, Joshua Hodges, Jeff Jewell, Marcia Larson, Ryan Mitchell, Erin Murello, Steve Murello, Alice Reeves, and Julie Siddique. Six participated in the second: Brock Ramos, Robert Thetford, Trait Thompson, Staci Thrasher, Shavonda Johnson, and Carlos Cruz-Fernandez. The twelve students participating in the third survey were Nathan Brown, Erin Ford, Paul Lore, Natalie Jackson, Christopher Murray, Sarah Norris, Thomas Rabovsky, Guanhai Song, Breanca Thomas, Sarah Trousset, Dustin Woods, and teaching assistant Natalie Jackson. The hard work, dedication, and intellectual contributions of those faculty and students were essential to the success of the surveys.

Julia Boortz, a student at the Massachusetts Institute of Technology, provided exceptional contributions to data analysis and the development of content for this report while an intern at CRS in 2010.

Doug Chapin and Sean Greene of the Election Reform Information Project (electionline.org) provided the original data set of local election officials.

Nearly 1,500 local election officials took the time from busy schedules to answer the many questions in the three surveys. The report would not have been possible without the thorough and thoughtful responses they made to the many survey questions

End Notes

[1] The surveys were designed for and sent to officials with primary responsibility for elections within a local jurisdiction—for example, a town clerk or county election director.

[2] For discussion of results from earlier surveys, see also CRS Report RL32938, *What Do Local Election Officials Think about Election Reform?: Results of a Survey*, by Eric A. Fischer and Kevin J. Coleman, and CRS Report RL34363, *Election Reform and Local Election Officials: Results of Two National Surveys*, by Eric A. Fischer and Kevin J. Coleman.

[3] In this report, the term *paper ballots* refers to hand-counted paper ballots. *Optical scan* is used to refer to PCOS and CCOS ballots, which are also composed of paper.

[4] Source: Election Reform Information Project, http://www.electionline.org.

[5] However, the increase observed in the survey data was not statistically significant (see the Appendix for an explanation of the statistical methods used). In this and other cases where the data were highly skewed toward one end of the distribution, the median (the midpoint of the distribution) from the LEO surveys is reported rather than the arithmetic mean, because the latter is more sensitive to extreme scores and therefore the median is generally considered a better measure of the average in such cases. The mean number of registered voters reported increased from about 40,000 in 2006 to 50,000 in 2008. Data on voters and polling places were not collected in the 2004 survey.

[6] According to one report, the number of registered voters nationwide was 189 million in 2008, an increase of 17.5 million, or 10%, from 2006 (Election Assistance Commission, *The Impact of the National Voter Registration Act of 1993 on the Administration of Elections for Federal Office 2007-2008: A Report to the 111th Congress*, June 30, 2009, http://www.eac.gov/assets The%20Impact%20of%20the%20National%20Voter%20Registration%20Act%20on%20Federal%20Elections%20200 7-2008.pdf, p. 1). Another study yielded a 7% increase (Michael P. McDonald, "2008 General Election Voter Registration Statistics," *United States Elections Project*, March 6, 2009, http://elections.gmu.edu/Registration_2008G.html).

[7] The median was 13 polling places in 2006 and 14 in 2008, with means of 32 and 37, respectively. The increase was not statistically significant. The minimum was zero because Oregon is a vote-by-mail state and does not generally use polling places. The maximum was about 1,000 in 2006 and about 1,700 in 2008. Not surprisingly, in each election the number of polling places in a jurisdiction was strongly correlated with the number of registered voters.

[8] This result is similar to the figure of 61% reported from an independent study in David C. Kimball and Martha Kropf, "The Street-Level Bureaucrats of Elections: Selection Methods for Local Election Officials," *Review of Policy Research* 23, no. 6 (2006): 1257-1268.

[9] Women make up about 60% of that workforce: see U.S. Census Bureau, "2000 Supplementary Survey Summary Table P068," available at http://factfinder.census.gov. Comparable data from the 2010 census were not available for this report.

[10] About 53% of the managers are men: see U.S. Census Bureau, "Census 2000 EEO Data Tool," available at http://www.census.gov/eeo2000/index.html.

[11] Ibid.

[12] Ibid.

[13] The cause of this change is not clear. However, the pattern is consistent with the contention by some observers that the changes in election administration brought about by HAVA could increase turnover.

[14] Many LEOs, for example, town clerks, have duties other than election administration.

[15] The proportion increased slightly for those who considered themselves "middle of the road" (34% in 2004 and 36% in 2008) or liberal (16% and 20%).

[16] The proportion is an estimate determined by comparing the number of LEOs who answered this question with the number answering the gender question, which was in the same section of the survey. Such a comparison was necessary because LEOs were asked only to indicate the organizations to which they belonged, not whether they belonged to any organization. The question on gender was chosen for the comparison because only a few LEOs answered the question on membership but not the question on gender, fewer than for other questions in that section of the survey. Using the percentage of total survey respondents would yield estimates of 60%-67%, but those are almost certainly underestimates.

[17] These questions were not asked in 2004 or 2008.

[18] Lever machines were used by 25% of townships in 2004, but none reported using them in 2008. As of 2011, lever machines were no longer used for voting in any U.S. election jurisdiction.

[19] Most of these declines were in counties, of which 10% used paper ballots in 2004 but only 2% in 2008, and 28% used CCOS in 2004 but 18% in 2008. The use of those two voting systems changed little in township jurisdictions, remaining at about 20% for paper ballots and 10% for CCOS.

[20] Both county and township use of PCOS increased, from 26% of counties in 2004 to 37% in 2008, and from 30% of townships in 2004 to 50% in 2008. DRE use remained at about 5% among townships, but increased from 22% to 35% in counties.

[21] See, for example, Election Data Services (EDS), "Nation Sees Drop in Use of Electronic Voting Equipment for 2008 Election—A First," October 17, 2008, http://www.edssurvey.com/images/. While the EDS report showed a similar small decrease in use of DREs by jurisdictions from 2006 to 2008, it also showed a larger decrease in use by voters, because jurisdictions that changed tended to be larger ones. Also, the EDS report provided results from all jurisdictions rather than a sample. However, it did not distinguish between central count and precinct-count optical scan systems.

[22] The results described here refer to the primary or main voting system used in a jurisdiction—the one that most voters would use. HAVA also requires that every polling place have at least one fully accessible voting system such as a properly equipped DRE. As a result, many jurisdictions using other kinds of voting systems also had one DRE per polling place.

[23] electionline.org, *Election Preview 2008* (Pew Center on the States, October 2008), http://www.pewcenteronthestates.org/uploadedFiles/Election%20Preview%20FINAL.pdf.

[24] Election Data Services, "Nation Sees Drop in Use of Electronic Voting." Most used punchcard, lever machine, and hand-counted paper systems.

[25] This problem had long been recognized. A 1988 National Bureau of Standards report called for the elimination of Votomatic pre-scored punch card voting, still in use in Palm Beach County, FL in the 2000 election. See Roy G. Saltman, *Accuracy, Integrity, and Security in Computerized Vote-Tallying*, NBS Special Publication 500-158 (National Bureau of Standards, August 1988), http://www.itl.nist.gov/lab/specpubs/500-158.htm.

[26] Many of the jurisdictions where LEOs chose "Other" may in fact use one of the three systems specified, but the description provided did not permit that determination (e.g., "paper" might mean a BMD).

[27] However, the results should be interpreted with some caution, since the rate of response to this question was relatively low—about 22% of survey respondents, whereas the median response rate to a specific question was 80%.

[28] Specifically, LEOs were asked about the statement, "Public interest groups/civil rights groups/advocates for the disabled have too great an influence on the process."

[29] Many respondents commented that they should not have been required by the federal government to change voting systems or to add accessible ones.

[30] Several questions in the 2004 survey were omitted in 2006 to make room for additional questions about election administration and the impacts of HAVA. Nevertheless, the 2006 survey had more than twice as many questions as the 2004 instrument. A smaller number of changes were made to the set of 2008 survey questions.

[31] Not surprisingly, the lowest interaction (13% of LEOs) was in paper-ballot jurisdictions, and the highest was in optical scan and DRE jurisdictions (about 85%).

[32] However, in the 2006 survey, about one in eight reported that vendors did not provide the expected level of support on election day (discussed later in this report).

[33] This question explored the views of LEOs about the concern that some observers have raised that the range of services vendors provide in some jurisdictions may amount to a kind of privatization of election administration.

[34] For this question, LEOs were also asked to rate their own influence, which received the highest average score. The question also asked about the influence of some other actors, such as courts and voters, and it listed elected and nonelected state and local officials but not election officials specifically, except the respondents themselves and the EAC.

[35] For this question, LEOs were asked to rank how they felt about the use of different types of voting systems for elections in the United States, on a scale of 1 (strongly oppose) to 7 (strongly support). The types of voting systems listed were lever machines, punchcard systems, hand-counted paper ballots, central-count optical scan, precinct-count optical scan, DRE, Internet, and other. Only 10% of LEOs supported Internet voting, and since this type of system has not been used in public elections in the United States (except experimentally on occasion), it is not discussed further in this report. The category "other" is not discussed because the response rate was very low (<5%).

[36] Nonusers of PCOS systems supported their use about as strongly as nonusers of CCOS systems supported their use. Nonusers were most strongly opposed to the use of punchcard systems, followed by lever machines and hand-counted paper ballots.

[37] Those states include Connecticut, Maine, New Hampshire, Oklahoma, Oregon, and Vermont (CRS analysis of data from Verified Voting, "The Verifier," 2010, http://www.verifiedvoting.org/verifier, supplemented by state sources).

[38] Too few jurisdictions used punchcards in 2006 and 2008 to permit meaningful statistical comparisons for this system.

[39] This conclusion is the result of a statistical comparison from a separate question and is not shown in the graph.

[40] The choices were punchcards, CCOS, DREs, hand-counted paper, PCOS, and Internet voting.

[41] The change seems surprising on its surface, because hand-marked optical scan ballots of either type are not accessible to persons with disabilities in the sense used in HAVA. However, some manufacturers have marketed accessible ballot-marking machines, and that could account for the increase.

[42] See CRS Report RL33190, *The Direct Recording Electronic Voting Machine (DRE) Controversy: FAQs and Misperceptions*, by Eric A. Fischer and Kevin J. Coleman.

[43] This conclusion is the result of a statistical comparison of responses from users of all voting systems in 2004 and is not shown in Figure 21.

[44] This conclusion is the result of a statistical comparison of responses from users of all voting systems in 2004 and is not shown in Figure 22.

[45] According to the EAC, 21 states used DREs without VVPAT in 2008, and 16 states used DREs with VVPAT (Election Assistance Commission, *The 2008 Election Administration and Voting Survey: A Summary of Key Findings*, November 2009, http://www.eac.gov/assets 2008%20Election%20Administration%20and%20Voting%20Survey%20EAVS%20Report.pdf). However, the EAC report did not present results at the level of local election jurisdictions.

[46] States increasingly offer absentee ballots to any voter requesting them, rather than requiring a reason such as disability or absence from the jurisdiction on election day.

[47] In the 2006 survey, only DRE users were asked if VVPAT should be required. All LEOs were asked that question in 2004 and 2008.

[48] In 2004, this question focused only on disadvantages, and in 2006, it was asked only of DRE users.

[49] This question was not asked in the other surveys.

[50] This question was not asked in the other surveys.

[51] The results on year-to-year differences hold despite a small inadvertent change in this question between the two surveys. In 2004, LEOs were asked to rate the difficulty on a scale of 0 (not difficult at all) to 10 (extremely difficult). In 2006, the scale began at 1. However, that change should have caused a slight increase, not a decrease, in the scores—the opposite of

the observed change for all but the two items discussed in the text. Normalizing the scores to a uniform scale did not change the described patterns significantly.

[52] The low rating for the compliance question is consistent with the decision by Congress not to grant the EAC regulatory authority.

[53] This question was asked only in 2006.

[54] There was a slight change in scale from 2006 (1-10) to 2008 (0-10), but the conclusions are unaffected, since the effect of the change was similar to that described for difficulty of HAVA implementation described in footnote 51.

[55] For some questions, LEOs were offered the opportunity to provide open-ended comments. For this question, LEOs were asked to make suggestions about ways to improve the EAC.

[56] The question in the two surveys varied slightly. The 2006 survey asked whether states had implemented a state-wide database, whereas the 2008 survey asked if they had fully complied with the requirement. As of 2010, California had still not complied (see CRS Report RS22505, *Voter Identification and Citizenship Requirements: Overview and Issues*, by Kevin J. Coleman and Eric A. Fischer), but some LEOs from 14 other states also believed their states had not fully complied by the time of the 2008 election.

[57] This question was not asked in 2008.

[58] This question was not asked in 2008.

[59] The number of LEOs who responded to these questions in 2006 was unusually small, because of an error in the survey instrument that caused most respondents to this question to be only those who answered the staffing question in the affirmative—about 250 respondents. More than 1,000 respondents answered these questions in 2008. Therefore, additional caution is warranted in interpreting the significance of the answers in 2006 and in comparing them between the two surveys. Nevertheless, the answers were fairly consistent.

[60] The question on security was asked in both surveys, and the answers were similar, although confidence was slightly lower in 2008. The question on contingency plans was asked only in 2006 and that on accuracy was asked only in 2008.

[61] The EAC reported that at least some jurisdictions in 19 states used electronic pollbooks in the 2008 election (Election Assistance Commission, *The 2008 Election Administration and Voting Survey*).

[62] For more information on this issue, see CRS Report RS22505, *Voter Identification and Citizenship Requirements: Overview and Issues*, by Kevin J. Coleman and Eric A. Fischer.

[63] See, for example, electionline.org, "Voter ID Laws," April 28, 2008, http://www.pewcenteronthestates.org/ uploadedFiles/voterID.laws.6.08.pdf.

[64] See, for example, Stephen Ansolabehere, *Access versus Integrity in Voter Identification Requirements*, VTP Working Paper #58 (Caltech/MIT Voting Technology Project, February 2007), http://www.votewps/vtp_wp58.pdf; Commission on Federal Election Reform, *Building Confidence in U.S. Elections*, September 2005, http://www1.american.edu/ia/cfer/report/full_report.pdf.

[65] This question was asked only in 2006.

[66] For more information on this issue, see CRS Report RS22505, *Voter Identification and Citizenship Requirements: Overview and Issues*, by Kevin J. Coleman and Eric A. Fischer.

[67] One HAVA requirement (§301(a)(3)(C)) went into effect January 1, 2007; it applies only to voting systems purchased with funds made available under title II after that date.

[68] In 2006, LEOs also stated that they worked an additional 20 hours per week in the month before the election. However, that question was not asked in 2008.

[69] Presumably, users of nonelectronic voting systems were reporting problems with their accessible voting systems, most of which are DREs or optical-scan systems with ballot-marking devices.

[70] A GAO survey of state election officials found that most states reported problems with voting systems during the 2006 election but that most problems had little impact (Government Accountability Office, *States, Territories, and the District Are Taking a Range of Important Steps to Manage Their Varied Voting System Environments*, GAO-08-874, September 2008, http://www.gao.gov/new.items/d08874.pdf).

[71] The survey asked LEOs to indicate only whether a particular event had occurred, not how many times. So if a DRE and precinct-count optical scan system have similar failure rates, then a jurisdiction using 1 DRE and 1 OS unit per polling place will probably have a lower incidence of failures than a jurisdiction that uses 10 DRE units per polling place. If the rate of failure per unit is 5%, the polling place using 1 OS and 1 DRE would have a 10% chance that at least one unit would fail, and the polling place using 10 DREs would have a 40% chance.

[72] For example, if the failure rate for DREs were 1% and that for OS 5%, a polling place using 1 OS and 1 DRE would have a 6% chance that at least one unit would fail, and the polling place using 10 DREs would have a 10% chance.

[73] Since many such users also use DREs to meet the HAVA accessibility requirements, it was not possible to determine whether it was an optical scan system or a DRE that the LEO assessed as having been hacked.

[74] This question was not asked in 2008.

[75] It was not possible to determine the ratio for actual voters, since LEOs were not asked how many of the registered voters participated in the election.

[76] It could not be determined if these numbers were significantly changed from 2006, because in 2008 LEOs were asked to list all the voting systems they used for early voting, whereas in 2006 they were asked to list only their primary system.

[77] Historically, most states have required voters to provide a reason such as illness, disability, or absence from the jurisdiction on election day as part of an application for an absentee ballot. However, most states now offer early voting, "no excuse" absentee voting, or both.

[78] This is essentially a form of early voting.

[79] The greater number of absentee ballots reported in 2008 without a corresponding increase in the percentage may be a result of the higher voter turnout in 2008.

[80] Election Assistance Commission, *The 2006 Election Administration and Voting Survey: A Summary of Key Findings,* December 2007, http://www.eac.gov/News/press/clearinghouse/2006-election-administration-and-voting-survey; ——, *The 2008 Election Administration and Voting Survey: A Summary of Key Findings*. The EAC reported a domestic civilian absentee-voting rate of 13.8% in 2006 and 16.6% in 2008, and an overseas-voter rate of 0.4% in 2006 and 0.5% in 2008.

[81] A ballot that a voter returns with whatever choices have been made is called a *voted ballot*.

[82] Those views were significantly correlated—that is, LEOs who believed that absentee voting should be a right were more likely to believe also that early voting should be.

[83] electionline.org, "Helping Americans Vote: Poll Workers," September 2007, http://www.electionline.org/Portals/1/ Publications/ERIPBrief19_final.pdf.

[84] The survey did not include questions on the age or number of hours worked by pollworkers.

[85] Note that this result does not mean that 20% of pollworkers did not understand their jobs, but that 20% of LEOs reported that lack of understanding had occurred often enough for them to consider it a problem.

[86] The median was more than 70.

[87] These averages reported here are medians, given the skewed distribution of these ratios.

[88] In 2006, respondents were given a choice of reporting daily or hourly wages. About 40% chose to report hourly compensation, which averaged $7.25.

[89] This result does not necessarily mean that no relationship exists, only that none was detected. While little research is available on this topic, available evidence supports the contention that training and performance are related (see, for example, Thad Hall, J. Quin Monson, and Kelly D. Patterson, "Poll Workers and the Vitality of Democracy: An Early Assessment," *PS: Political Science and Politics*, Vol. XL(4), October 2007, p. 647-654, available at http://www.vote

[90] In both surveys, the mean was about 3.25, the median 3, the mode 2, and the maximum 36.

[91] This question was asked only in 2006.

[92] This question was asked only in 2006.

[93] R. Michael Alvarez, Lonna Rae Atkeson, and Thad E. Hall, *The New Mexico Election Administration Report: The 2006 November General Election,* August 2, 2007, p. 20, available at http://www.voteNM_Election_Report_8-07.pdf.

[94] This question was asked only in 2006.

[95] Title V authorized grants for the college program created, and Title VI established a federally chartered foundation for the high school program.

[96] However, in 2006 more than half of elected LEOs (57%) indicated that they communicated their party affiliation during their election. This question was not asked in 2008. According to another study prior to the 2006 election, about one-fifth of local jurisdictions were administered by Republicans and one-quarter by Democrats, with about two-fifths nonpartisan and the remainder bipartisan (Kimball and Kropf, "Street-Level Bureaucrats," p. 1262).

[97] For example, Maine ranks 37th among states in population, with 1.3 million residents, but it ranks 4th in the number of election jurisdictions, with 518.

[98] For discussion of the DRE security issue and proposals for resolving it, see CRS Report RL33190, *The Direct Recording Electronic Voting Machine (DRE) Controversy: FAQs and Misperceptions*, by Eric A. Fischer and Kevin J. Coleman; and CRS Report RL32139, *Election Reform and Electronic Voting Systems (DREs): Analysis of Security Issues*, by Eric A. Fischer.

[99] The Government Accountability Office surveyed a sample of about 600 LEOs nationwide by mail and about 160 by telephone following the 2000 federal election (see Government Accountability Office, *Elections: Perspectives on Activities and Challenges Across the Nation,* GAO-02-3, October 2001). That survey focused largely on issues of election management, such as the availability of poll workers and the processing of absentee ballots. While results of the two surveys are not generally comparable because of differences in focus and methodology, the GAO survey did find that a high percentage of local officials expressed satisfaction with the performance of their existing voting systems, a finding consistent with the results of the current survey.

[100] See the section on acknowledgements at the end of this report.

[101] The authors wish to thank the many people who devoted time and energy to this project. Most important among them were nearly 1,500 local election officials who took the time from busy schedules to answer the many questions in the two surveys. Doug Chapin and Sean Greene of the Election Reform Information Project (electionline.org) provided the original data set of local election officials. The skills and dedication of the principal investigators

and students at Texas A&M University were essential to the successful completion of the project.

[102] Individual responses were anonymous, in keeping with human-subjects research requirements for the surveys. Those requirements prevented the inclusion of the District of Columbia, which has only one LEO.

[103] The number of LEOs per state varies greatly, from fewer than 10 to more than 1,000. The number varies much more strongly with the way states have chosen to organize their election jurisdictions than it does with variables such as the voting-age populations of the states. Consequently, a simple random sample of the total number of election officials in the United States would have caused states with more decentralized election administration to be disproportionately represented in the set of responses. Alternative approaches that attempted to weight the data (by state, voting-age population, or portion of LEOs, for example) would also have had weaknesses in addressing questions of representativeness. There is no simple solution to this problem, and the sampling strategy used in the two surveys was chosen as a way to strike a reasonable balance between populational and geographic representation. In combination with the unweighted statistical analyses performed for this report, the strategy has the effect of increasing the relative influence of the four-fifths of states with fewer than 150 LEOs while ensuring a relatively strong influence of states with large numbers of LEOs.

[104] This number is for questions that applied to all LEOs. Some questions were targeted to specific groups, such as users of DREs.

[105] In each survey, the choices for kind of jurisdiction were county, town, township, borough, and other. In 2006, LEOs could write in the kind of jurisdiction they administered in the "other" category, and almost all of those indicated their jurisdiction as a city. The option to write in a response did not exist in the 2004 survey, and the pattern of response strongly suggests that most LEOs with city jurisdictions chose "town" or "township" as the most closely matching category.

[106] This was only an issue for those few questions where LEOs provided "ad-lib" answers rather than choosing from among a range of options.

[107] For example, when asked how many additional hours per week LEOs worked in the four weeks preceding the election, the responses of five LEOs presented in the database as impossibly large numbers such as 1015 or 2530 (there are 168 hours in a week). Those responses were clearly incorrect. Given the structure of those responses, the intent was interpreted as a range, 10-15 and 25-30 in the examples, and the number of hours was corrected to the midpoint of the range, 12.5 and 27.5.

In: Voting and Election Reform
Editor: Nicole P. Fletcher
ISBN: 978-1-61324-640-5

Chapter 2

THE HELP AMERICA VOTE ACT AND ELECTIONS REFORM: OVERVIEW AND ISSUES*

Kevin J. Coleman and Eric A. Fischer

SUMMARY

Since the November 2000 presidential election, previously obscure details of voting and vote counting have been the focus of ongoing public attention and legislative action at the state and federal levels. The Help America Vote Act (HAVA, P.L. 107-252) was enacted in October 2002, and the states have made additional changes to election laws and procedures since then. Numerous bills to amend HAVA have been considered in the Congress as well, although only one has been enacted that made a minor change to the law. HAVA created a new federal agency (the Election Assistance Commission), set requirements for various aspects of election administration, and provided federal funding. However, the law did not supplant state and local control over election administration.

In the 112th Congress, H.R. 235 includes provisions that would terminate, upon enactment, the Election Assistance Commission's (EAC) authority to make requirements payments to the states, rescind

* This is an edited, reformatted and augmented version of a Congressional Research Services publication, CRS Report for Congress RS20898, from www.crs.gov, dated January 13, 2011.

unobligated requirements payments as of enactment, and terminate the EAC.

The 111th Congress enacted a new military and overseas citizens voting law that was signed into law in October 2009 as part of the defense authorization act (P.L. 111-84). The House passed H.R. 512, which would prohibit a state's chief election official from actively participating in a federal election campaign, unless the official or an immediate family member was the candidate. The bill passed the House on September 29, 2010, but died in the Senate. A number of election reform bills were reported in the House as well. The reported bills would have established universal absentee voting (H.R. 1604), provided grants for voluntary absentee ballot tracking (H.R. 2510), and made improvements to military voting procedures (H.R. 2393).

For FY2011, the President's budget request includes $16.8 million for the EAC but does not include new funding for election reform payments to the states. The Senate Appropriations Committee (S.Rept. 111-238) and the House Financial Services and General Government Appropriations Subcommittee recommended the same amount for the EAC, with no election reform payments to the states. The EAC has been operating under FY2010 funding levels since September 30, 2010, when the first (P.L. 111-242) of four continuing resolutions was signed into law. The second through the fourth continuing resolutions extended the expiration date of P.L. 111-242, now set to expire on March 4, 2011.

For FY2010, the President's budget request included $16.5 million for the Election Assistance Commission (EAC) and $106 million for election reform payments to states. The House and Senate bills (H.R. 3170, S. 1432) would have provided about the same amount for the EAC; the House bill would have provided nearly the same amount for election payments, while the Senate bill called for $52 million in election payments. The Consolidated Appropriations Act (H.R. 3288), which was signed by the President on December 16, 2009, included $17.9 million for the EAC and $75 million for election reform programs.

In the 110th Congress, election reform issues included HAVA funding, paper audit trails for electronic voting systems, military and overseas voting, and deceptive practices and voter intimidation in elections. The House approved two bills and the Senate approved one, but none were enacted. The House passed H.R. 1281, the Deceptive Practices and Voter Intimidation Prevention Act of 2007, on June 25, 2008, and H.R. 6625, the Veteran Voting Support Act, on September 17. The Senate passed S. 3073, the Military Voting Protection Act of 2008, on October 1, 2008.

THE HELP AMERICA VOTE ACT

Even before the 2000 presidential election had been resolved by the U.S. Supreme Court in December of that year, more than a dozen bills to reform the election process had been introduced in the Congress. Legislative activity continued when the 107th Congress convened the following month, along with the release of various independent reports and studies on election reform. In December 2001, the House passed H.R. 3295, the Help America Vote Act. The Senate passed S. 565, the Martin Luther King, Jr. Equal Protection of Voting Rights Act, in early 2002, after adopting 40 amendments. Following conference negotiations, the compromise bill, the Help America Vote Act of 2002 (HAVA, P.L. 107-252) was enacted in October.

HAVA imposed a number of requirements on the states with respect to election administration, provided payments to the states to meet the new requirements, created the Election Assistance Commission, made changes to improve military and overseas voting, and authorized other election reform activities. Among its major provisions, HAVA did the following:

- created the Election Assistance Commission (EAC), an independent, bipartisan agency to carry out grant programs, provide for testing and certification of voting systems, study election issues, and issue guidelines for voting systems and the act's requirements;
- established a number of payment and grant programs to help states meet the law's requirements; replace punchcard and lever voting machines and make general election improvements; promote accessibility in the electoral process; promote student participation; and support pilot programs;
- established requirements in the states to provide a provisional ballot to a voter who is not on the registration list or whose registration is in question; post a sample ballot and voter information at polling places on election day; impose an identification standard for first-time voters who register by mail; provide for voter error correction on voting systems used in federal elections; provide for manual auditing of the voting system, alternative-language accessibility, and at least one machine per voting place that can provide disability access; and create and maintain a computerized, verified statewide voter registration list;
- required the EAC to develop voting system guidelines for computer hardware and software for voluntarily use by the states, and voluntary guidance to assist states in meeting the requirements;

- left methods of implementation to the states and prohibited rulemaking by the EAC, leaving enforcement to the U.S. Attorney General while requiring states to establish grievance procedures; and
- amended the Uniformed and Overseas Citizens Absentee Voting Act (UOCAVA) to make improvements to voting procedures for members of the military and overseas citizens.

Although many bills have been introduced to amend HAVA since it became law, only a minor change has been enacted. The National Defense Authorization Act for 2010 made numerous amendments to UOCAVA and also amended HAVA to authorize appropriations to achieve compliance on the new military and overseas voting requirements.

VOTING SYSTEMS AND ELECTION ADMINISTRATION

While initial reactions after the 2000 election had tended to focus on technological fixes such as eliminating punchcards, a consensus emerged subsequently that the issues, and the solutions needed, were more complex and often involved trade-offs among diverse goals. HAVA reflects those developments—it funded replacement of punchcard and lever systems but also broader improvements in election administration.

Voting Systems

Currently, most jurisdictions use one of two kinds of voting system:

- *optical scan,* in which voters mark choices on paper ballots by hand or machine and the ballots are read by an electronic counting device, or
- *direct recording electronic (DRE) systems,* in which voters mark choices via a computer interface and the voting machine records them directly to an electronic memory.

There is no consensus on whether any one technology is best. Use of optical scan and DRE systems increased after the enactment of HAVA, and these systems are now used by 90% of voters. States have different practices and requirements. HAVA does not require any particular voting system, but it sets requirements that influence what systems election officials choose. Systems used in federal elections must provide for error correction by voters, manual auditing, accessibility, alternative languages, and error-rate standards. Systems must also maintain voter privacy and ballot confidentiality, and states must adopt uniform standards for what constitutes a vote on each system.

In September 2009, ES&S, considered by many to be the largest voting-system vendor in the United States, announced that it had acquired Premier Election Solutions, considered the second largest. This acquisition raised concerns among some other vendors, election officials, and activists. A particular concern was whether the larger market share the acquisition gave ES&S would create a monopolistic environment in the voting-system industry. The merger announcement prompted a lawsuit by competitor Hart Intercivic against ES&S and Diebold, Incorporated, Premier's parent company, on antitrust grounds, and led to an investigation and lawsuit by the U.S. Department of Justice. The case was settled in March 2010 with an agreement by ES&S to divest specified assets acquired from Premier.

Electronic Voting Machine Controversy

HAVA's requirement for accessible voting systems (at least one per polling place) and other factors drove some states to adopt DREs, but controversy exists about the security of those systems. Some experts and advocates believe that the problem is serious enough to require that all voting systems produce paper ballots that can be verified by voters and that will serve as the official record of the votes for any recount. Others believe that other safeguards can make DREs sufficiently safe from tampering, that use of printed paper ballots would create too many problems, and that the controversy risks drawing attention away from the demonstrated utility of DREs in addressing problems of access to and usability of voting systems. HAVA requires a paper audit trail for the voting system, but not paper ballots. However, many states have instituted paper-ballot-trail requirements.

Several bills introduced in recent Congresses would address this issue. Most would require a specific design standard for paper ballots rather than setting a performance standard that can be met in different ways, which was the approach taken by HAVA with respect to voting system requirements. Proponents of paper ballots argue that a legislated design standard is the only way to ensure that voting systems exhibit the desired level of verifiability and security. Opponents argue that such a design standard freezes technology and stifles innovation, thereby precluding the development and implementation of technologies with superior levels of verifiability and security than is possible with current technology.[1]

Federal Funding

A central issue has been the role of the federal government in addressing concerns about voting systems, particularly with respect to funding and standards. HAVA authorized $3.86 billion in funding for programs to replace equipment, improve election administration, improve accessibility, recruit pollworkers, and perform research and pilot studies. The amount appropriated by Congress thus far is $3.54 billion. (See "Funding Under the Help America Vote Act" below.)

Election Assistance Commission

Before HAVA, federal activities relating to election administration were performed by the Office of Election Administration (OEA) of the Federal Election Commission (FEC). Other than the voluntary voting system standards, OEA performed clearinghouse functions and some administrative activities under the National Voter Registration Act (P.L. 103-31). HAVA replaced the OEA with the Election Assistance Commission (EAC, http://www.eac.gov), an independent, bipartisan federal agency. The act also established two boards, with broad-based state and local membership, and a technical committee, to address aspects of voting system standards and certification. The statute also provides for technical support and participation by the National Institute of Standards and Technology (NIST, see http://vote. The EAC carries out grant programs, provides for testing and certification of voting systems, studies election issues, and issues voluntary guidelines for voting systems and guidance for the requirements in the act. The EAC has no rule-making authority (except for limited authority under the National Voter Registration Act of 1993, the "motor-voter" law) and does not enforce HAVA requirements. The act established two enforcement processes: the U.S. Attorney General may bring civil action with respect to HAVA requirements, and states, as a condition for receipt of funds, were required to establish administrative grievance procedures to handle complaints from individuals.

HAVA authorized appropriations for the EAC for FY2003 through FY2005, and it has been funded in each fiscal year since FY2005, as well. At least one bill was introduced to make the EAC a permanent agency (H.R. 550, 109th Congress). In the 111th Congress, an amendment (S.Amdt. 4764) to the Airport and Airway Extension Act of 2010, Part III (H.R. 4853) was offered that would have eliminated the Election Assistance Commission, but the amendment was not adopted. In the 112th Congress, H.R. 235 (Representative Kevin Brady) would terminate the EAC and its authority to make requirements payments to the states and would rescind unobligated requirements payments. No amounts could be expended after enactment, except to terminate ongoing projects and activities that use requirements payments or those necessary to terminate commission activities and projects.

Standards and Requirements

In the 1980s, the FEC developed voluntary standards for computer-based voting systems. Most states have now adopted those standards, which were updated in 2002. HAVA codifies the development and regular updating of those standards, which it calls voluntary guidelines. The EAC issued draft guidelines for public comment in June 2005. The final version took effect in December 2007. A new, completely rewritten draft version was released for public review in October 2007.[2] HAVA also establishes federal requirements for voting systems, registration, provisional ballots, and other aspects of election administration. It leaves the methods of implementation to the states but requires the EAC to issue voluntary guidance.[3]

Voter Identification

The Help America Vote Act requires that certain voters who had registered by mail present a form of identification from a list specified in the act. States vary greatly in what identification they require voters to present, ranging from nothing beyond the federal requirement to photographic identification for all voters. A number of states enacted laws in recent years to require photo ID to vote, which resulted in a series of state court challenges and rulings. In the 109th Congress, the House passed legislation to require photo identification and proof of citizenship when voting in federal elections, but no further action followed. The U.S. Supreme Court has upheld an Indiana statute requiring photo identification for voting.[4]

Voter Registration

With the passage of HAVA, Congress attempted to address voter registration problems by requiring computerization and integration of voter registration systems and placing primary responsibility at the state level of government. That requirement went into effect in January 2006. The absence of a clear national standard for the HAVA-required statewide systems has led to uncertainties about how states should develop them and even whether states will be able to meet the requirements. Given the problems some states have had, the increase in new-voter registration in recent elections, and recent closely contested presidential elections, issues associated with voter registration systems have become more prominent. Among them are questions about the integrity and accuracy of the new statewide systems, the validity of new registrations, concerns about various kinds of fraud and abuse, and the impacts of attempts to challenge the validity of voters' registrations at polling places.

FUNDING UNDER THE HELP AMERICA VOTE ACT

States and territories were eligible to receive $2.3 billion in federal requirements payments under HAVA, once each jurisdiction had published a "state plan" in the *Federal Register*, followed by a 45-day public comment period and the filing of a certification with the EAC. The state plans were published on March 24, 2004. The $2.3 billion included funds appropriated in FY2003 and FY2004, which could not be allocated until establishment of the EAC and publication of the state plans. The EAC distributed all of that funding to states by December 2005; no additional funding for requirements payments was appropriated until FY2008, when $115 million was appropriated. An additional $100 million was appropriated for FY2009. Payments have been distributed to states and territories to meet the new HAVA requirements and can be used for general election administration improvements once the requirements have been met.

HAVA established the following payment and grant programs (see *Table 1* below for authorized and appropriated amounts):

- *Election Administration Improvements.* Provided expedited, one-time formula payments for general election administration improvements to states that applied, with a $5 million minimum combined payment per state for this and the replacement program (see next paragraph). Administered by General Services Administration (GSA). (Sec. 101.)

- *Replacement of Punchcard and Lever Machine Systems.* Provided expedited, one-time formula payments to replace punchcard systems and lever machines in qualifying states, with a $5 million minimum combined payment per state for this and the improvements program, summarized above. Administered by GSA. (Sec. 102.)
- *Payments to Meet Election Requirements.* Provides annual formula payments to states to meet the act's requirements. Requires a 5% match and submission of a state plan. Administered by the Election Assistance Commission (EAC) created in the act. (Sec. 251-258.)
- *Payments to Assure Accessibility.* Provides payments to states to make polling places accessible to persons with disabilities. Requires application. Administered by Department of Health and Human Services (HHS). (Sec. 265-265.)
- *Payments for Protection and Advocacy Systems.* Provides payments to state protection and advocacy systems to ensure electoral participation by persons with disabilities. Requires application. Administered by HHS. (Sec. 291-292.)
- *Grants for Research and Pilot Programs.* Provides grants for research to improve voting technology (Sec. 271-273) and for pilot programs to test new voting technology (Sec. 281-283). Requires application. Administered by EAC.
- *Student Programs.* Establishes three programs, one to recruit college students as pollworkers (Sec. 501-503), one to recruit high school students (Sec. 601), and one to provide grants for the National Student and Parent Mock Election (Sec. 295-296).

Appropriations

The FY2003 omnibus appropriations bill (H.J.Res. 2, H.Rept. 108-10, P.L. 108-7), signed into law on February 20, 2003, contained $1.5 billion for election reform programs authorized by HAVA, including $650 million combined for the election administration improvement and voting system replacement payments to be administered by GSA (with no specific allocation designated for either program and a maximum of $500,000 for administrative costs). GSA disbursed all of these funds to states in June 2003. All states and territories received payments for election administration improvements, based on a formula using each state's voting-age population, and payments to replace punch card and lever voting systems were made to all states that applied. Also included was $830 million for requirements payments (with a maximum of 0.1% to be paid to any territory), and $20 million for other programs—$13 million for accessibility payments, $2 million for protection and advocacy programs, $1.5 million each for the college and high school programs, and $2 million for the EAC. P.L. 108-7 also included a $15 million appropriation to GSA for one-time payments to certain states that had obtained optical scan or electronic voting systems prior to the November 2000 election.

The President's budget request for FY2004 included $500 million, one-half the amount authorized, to fund EAC requirements payments and administration. No funds were specifically requested for the other programs described above. The final omnibus appropriations bill, H.R. 2673, signed into law on January 23, 2004 (P.L. 108-199), contained just over $1.5 billion for election reform, including $1.0 billion for requirements payments, $500 million for election reform programs, $10 million for accessibility payments, $5 million for protection and advocacy systems, and $1.2 million for the EAC.

For FY2005, the President's budget request included $65 million for election reform, of which $40 million was additional funding for requirements payments and $10 million was for EAC administrative expenses. The request also included $5 million for protection and advocacy programs and $10 million for accessibility payments. The omnibus appropriations bill for FY2005, H.R. 4818, was signed into law on December 8, 2004, and included $14 million for the EAC, of which $2.8 million was to be transferred to NIST, and $15 million for disability voting access, with $5 million of that amount to apply to protection and advocacy systems. Also included was $200,000 for the student parent mock election program and $200,000 for the Help America Vote College Program.

The President's FY2006 budget request included $17.6 million for the EAC (of which $2.8 million is for NIST), as well as $5 million for protection and advocacy programs and $9.9 million for accessibility payments administered by HHS. The final appropriation (P.L. 109-115) contained $14.2 million, including $2.8 million for NIST, with $13.5 and $8.6 million, respectively, for the HHS programs, and $250,000 "encouraged" to be spent on the Help America Vote College Program.

The FY2007 request included $16.9 million for the EAC ($5 million for NIST), $4.83 million for protection and advocacy programs, and $10.89 million for accessibility payments administered by HHS. The 109th Congress adjourned without enacting an appropriations measure, providing instead temporary funding until February 15, 2007, via a continuing resolution (H.J.Res. 102). Continued funding through September 30 for FY2007 was subsequently provided via another continuing resolution, H.J.Res. 20, which was signed by the President on February 15 (P.L. 110- 5). It provided $16.24 million for the EAC, of which $4.95 million was for NIST, $4.83 million for protection and advocacy programs, and $10.89 million for disability access.

The FY2008 request included $15.5 million for the EAC ($3.25 million for NIST), and $4.83 million for protection and advocacy programs and $10.89 million for accessibility payments administered by HHS. From the start of FY2008 until December 31, 2007, continued funding for the EAC was provided by a series of continuing resolutions. Ultimately, FY2008 funding was provided by the Consolidated Appropriations Act for 2008, enacted on December 16, 2007 (P.L. 110-161). It provided $16.53 million for the EAC, of which $3.25 million is for NIST, and $200,000 is for the student and parent mock election program. It also provided $115 million for requirements payments, $10 million for data collection grants to selected states, $4.83 million for protection and advocacy programs, and $12.37 million for disability access.

The FY2009 request included $16.68 million for the EAC (with $4 million for NIST), as well as $5.26 million for protection and advocacy programs and $12.15 million for accessibility payments administered by HHS. The FY2009 appropriations were provided initially in a continuing resolution (P.L. 110-329), which provided the same funding levels as FY2008, and then in an omnibus bill (P.L. 111-8) that was passed on March 11, 2009. The omnibus provided $18 million for the EAC, with $4 million of that to be transferred to NIST, $750,000 for the College Program, and $300,000 for the high school mock election program. It also provided funding for requirements payments to the states in the amount of $100 million, with an additional $5 million for grants for research on voting technology improvements and $1 million for a pilot program for grants to states and localities to test voting systems before and after elections. Finally, the omnibus provided $12.2 million for disability access and $5.3 million for protection and advocacy programs.

Table 1. Help America Vote Act (HAVA) Funding
($ millions)

Budget Item	HAVA Auth.[a]	Appropriations								
		2003	2004	2005	2006	2007	2008	2009	2010	Total
Payments to States										
Election Administration Improvement	325	650[b]								650
Punchcard/Lever Machine Replacement	325									
HAVA Requirements	3,000	830	1,498				115	100	70	2,613
One-Time Payment[c]		15								15
Total Payments[d]	3,650	1,495	1,498				115	100	70	3,278
Election Assistance Commission (EAC)										
General[e]	30.00	2.00	2.00	10.71	11.29	11.29	23.08[f]	14.00	13.41	87.77
NIST				2.78	2.77	4.95	3.25	4.00	3.50	21.25
College Program	5.00[g]	1.50	0.75	0.20	0.00[h]			0.80	0.75	4.00
High School Program	5.00[g]	1.50	0.75							2.25
Mock Election	0.20[g]		0.20	0.20			0.20	0.30	0.30	1.20
Research	20.00							5.00	3.00	5.00
Pilot Programs	10.00							1.00	2.00	1.00
Total EAC	70.20	5.00	3.70	13.88	14.06	16.24	26.53	25.10	22.96	127.47

Budget Item	HAVA Auth.[a]	Appropriations								
		2003	2004	2005	2006	2007	2008	2009	2010	Total
Health and Human Services (HHS)										
Accessibility	100.00	13.00	10.00	10.00	10.90	10.90	12.40	12.20	12.15	91.55
Protection and Advocacy	40.00g	2.00	5.00	4.96	4.83	4.83	5.35	5.30	5.26	37.52
Total HHS	140.00	15.00	15.00	14.96	15.73	15.73	17.75	17.50	17.41	129.08
Total HAVA	3,860	1,515	1,517	29	30	32	159	143	110	3,535

Source: CRS, from HAVA and relevant appropriations acts.

Notes: All figures are in millions of current (nominal) dollars of budget authority as authorized or appropriated and are rounded where necessary. Figures for FY2005 and FY2006 include rescissions.

[a] Authorization amounts in HAVA.

[b] Appropriated amount did not specify the distribution of funds between the two budget items.

[c] For payments to states that had obtained optical scan or DRE voting systems prior to the November 2000 election. The funds were appropriated in the General Government and Appropriations Act of 2003, whereas payments to states authorized under HAVA were appropriated in the Miscellaneous Appropriations Act of 2003; both acts were included as divisions of the FY2003 omnibus appropriations act, P.L. 108-7.

[d] The total payment appropriated includes the one-time payment in FY2003 and is therefore $15 million greater than the total appropriated from funds authorized by HAVA. See note c.

[e] Figures in this row are funds remaining in EAC line items after amounts for other specific items (such as NIST) are subtracted.

[f] This includes $10 million for grants of $2 million each to five states to improve the collection of election data.

[g] Listed amounts plus sums necessary for subsequent years beyond the initial authorization period.

[h] Congress appropriated no funds for this in FY2006 but "encouraged" the EAC to spend $250,000 on it.

For FY2010, the President's budget request included $16.5 million for the Election Assistance Commission (EAC) and $106 million for election reform payments to states, with $5.26 million for protection and advocacy programs and $12.15 million for accessibility payments administered by HHS, as in FY2009. The House and Senate bills (H.R. 3170, S. 1432) would have provided about the same amount for the EAC. The House bill would have provided nearly the same amount for election payments, while the Senate bill called for $52 million in election payments. The Consolidated Appropriations Act, 2010 (P.L. 111-117) that was signed into law on December 16, 2009, includes $18.0 million for the EAC, of which $3.5 million is to be transferred to NIST, $750,000 is for the Help America Vote College Program, and $300,000 is for a competitive grant program to support student and parent mock elections. It also includes $75 million for election reform programs, with $70 million of that amount for requirements payments, $3 million for research grants to improve voting technology with respect to disability access, and $2 million for grants to states and localities for voting system logic and accuracy testing. Also, the omnibus provided $12.15 million for disability access and $5.26 million for protection and advocacy programs.

For FY2011, the President's budget request includes $16.8 million for the EAC, of which $3.25 million is to be transferred to NIST. It also includes $5.26 million for protection and advocacy programs and $12.15 million for accessibility payments administered by HHS. It includes EAC "election reform grants" among programs to be terminated, and therefore provides no funding for requirements payments, research and pilot program grants, the college program, and mock elections. As justification, it points out that about $1 billion in EAC payments to states remains unspent and claims that states have accrued $763 million in interest on previously appropriated payments. The EAC, in contrast, lists accrued interest through 2008 as totaling $279 million. The cause of this discrepancy is not clear. Funding for federal agencies, including the EAC, has been provided at FY2010 levels according to a continuing resolution, P.L. 111-242, since it was enacted on September 30, 2010. Three subsequent continuing resolutions further extended funding for the federal government through March 4, 2011.

LEGISLATION

In the 111th Congress, the House passed a bill that would have prohibited certain electoral activity by each state's chief election administration official.

H.R. 512 was passed on September 29, 2010, and would have prohibited such officials from actively taking part in a federal political campaign unless the official or an immediate family member was the candidate. In addition, a new military and overseas citizens voting law was enacted in October 2009. The new law originated in the Senate as S. 1415, which was reported with amendments by the Senate Rules Committee in July 2009. It was passed in October 2009 as an amendment to the National Defense Authorization Act of 2010 (P.L. 111-84), and it amends the Uniformed and Overseas Citizens Absentee Voting Act (UOCAVA; P.L. 99-410) to allow for electronic and mail transmission of voting materials, requires that states send out absentee ballots at least 45 days before an election, requires collection and delivery of overseas military ballots, and requires other improvements. In other legislative action, the House Administration Committee reported three bills, H.R. 1604 and H.R. 2510, both sponsored by Representative Susan Davis, and H.R. 2393, sponsored by Representative Kevin McCarthy. H.R. 1604 would have extended no-excuse absentee voting by mail (a voter does not need to provide an excuse to vote absentee) to all states and H.R. 2510 would have reimbursed states for the cost of establishing a voluntary, absentee ballot tracking program. H.R. 2393 would have required the Secretary of Defense to collect absentee ballots from overseas military voters for express delivery (a similar provision was enacted in P.L. 111- 84) and made other improvements to UOCAVA.

End Notes

[1] See CRS Report RL33190, The Direct Recording Electronic Voting Machine (DRE) Controversy: FAQs and Misperceptions.

[2] See CRS Report RS21156, Federal Voting Systems Standards and Guidelines: Congressional Deliberations; and CRS Report RL33146, Federal Voluntary Voting System Guidelines: Summary and Analysis of Issues.

[3] See CRS Report RL32685, Election Reform: The Help America Vote Act and Issues for Congress.

[4] See CRS Report RS22882, The Constitutionality of Requiring Photo Identification for Voting: An Analysis of Crawford v. Marion County Election Board.

In: Voting and Election Reform
Editor: Nicole P. Fletcher
ISBN: 978-1-61324-640-5

Chapter 3

THE NATIONAL VOTER REGISTRATION ACT OF 1993: HISTORY, IMPLEMENTATION, AND EFFECTS*

Royce Crocker

SUMMARY

After the passage of the Voting Rights Act of 1965 (42 U.S.C. § 1973–1973aa-6, see http://www.law.cornell.edu/uscode/html/ uscode 42/usc_sup 01 42 10 20 20 I-A.html), legislation had been urged for over two decades that would create a national voter registration system designed to make registration easier and more uniform from state to state. The National Voter Registration Act of 1993 (NVRA, P.L. 103-31, 107 Stat.77, [42 U.S.C. § 1973gg et seq., see http://www.law.cornell. edu/uscode/ html/ uscode42/usc_sup 01 42 10 20 20 I-H.html]), the so-called "motor-voter" bill, was signed into law by President Clinton on May 20, 1993. It required states to establish voter registration procedures for federal elections so that eligible citizens might apply to register to vote (1) simultaneously while applying for a driver's license, (2) by mail, and (3) at selected state and local offices that serve the public. The law took effect on January 1, 1995, for most states.

---

* This is an edited, reformatted and augmented version of a Congressional Research Services publication, CRS Report for Congress R40609, from www.crs.gov, dated September 9, 2009.

Proponents argued that the NVRA would make it easier to register to vote, provide more-thanadequate measures to prevent voter fraud by making violations a federal offense, and cost states very little to implement, based on the experiences of states that previously used some form of "motor-voter" registration.

Opponents, on the other hand, argued that there was little evidence that increasing the number of persons on voter registration rolls would lead to higher voter turnout. By making it so easy to register, they believed the act would increase the likelihood of election fraud. Furthermore, according to opponents, implementation would be costly to the states, in terms both of dollars and other administrative costs.

The NVRA has been the law of the land for 16 years and has been in effect for 14 years. Between 1992 and 2008, voter registration increased nationally by almost nine percentage points. The courts have resolved many of the initial issues. A review of the required NVRA reports appears to indicate that the states have come to terms with the provisions, despite the fact that they would still like the federal government to provide funding for the implementation of aspects of the act. While amending parts of the NVRA in minor ways, the Help America Vote Act, passed in 2002, also created additional voter registration demands on the states (HAVA, P.L. 107-252 [42 U.S.C., Subchapter III, Part A., § 15482(a), 15483, see http://www.law.cornell.edu/uscode/html/uscode42/ usc_sup_ 01_42_10_146_20_III_30_A.html; 15532, see http://www.law. cornell.edu/ uscode/html/uscode42/usc_sec_42_00015532----000-.html]).

However, there are still some problems with implementation at the local levels and in some selected state agencies, as well as with the training of non-election officials who are responsible under the NVRA for providing voter registration services. Some would like to curtail parts of the NVRA. Some do not think the NVRA has gone far enough.

This report provides an historical background for voter registration reform and the NVRA, a description of the major aspects of the act, a discussion of the implementation and post-implementation actions, and a catalog of subsequent efforts to amend or repeal the act.

INTRODUCTION

After the 2008 presidential election, concerns were raised about problems with voter registration procedures in several states. Issues such as failure to register persons at designated state voter registration agencies (state offices dealing with social services and disabilities), lack of training among non-election administration personnel responsible for registering potential voters and requirements for the registration of eligible college students were highlighted as specific concerns.[1]

The Justice Department has come under criticism recently for not fully enforcing the National Voter Registration Act of 1993 (NVRA, P.L. 103-31) during the George W. Bush Administration. And, more recently, the Chairman of the Senate Rules and Administration Committee, Senator Charles Schumer, in hearings in April 2009, pressed Attorney General Eric Holder to "pull out all the stops" and sue any state not complying with the agency-based provisions of the NVRA. If the 111th Congress chooses to address these issues, the NVRA may be the subject of debate and amendment.

BACKGROUND

Efforts to establish a national voter registration system followed closely on the heels of passage of the Voting Rights Act in 1965. In the early 1970s, a substantial effort was made to establish a national "postcard" or mail registration system. In the 92nd Congress, both the Senate and the House held hearings on a proposal to establish a national voter registration system, with the Census Bureau conducting postcard registration for federal elections. The proposal came to the Senate floor for a vote but was tabled. In the 93rd Congress, both the Senate and the House again considered much the same proposal; a national postcard voter registration system, administered by a new National Voter Registration Administration located in the Census Bureau. The Senate passed the bill (S. 352, S. Rept. 93-91) May 9, 1973 (vote: 57-37). The House, on May 8, 1974, refused to take up the bill (H.R. 8053, H. Rept. 93-778) to establish a national postcard voter registration system by rejecting the rule under which the measure was to be debated on the floor (vote:197-204). In 1975, the House passed a modified version of the postcard voter registration measure, eliminating the required mass mailing of postcards to every household; the postcards were to be made available at post offices and other public offices (H.R. 11552; August 9, 1975, H. Rept. 94-798, vote: 239-147). The measure, however, stalled in the Senate.

During the first year of the Carter presidency, reform efforts focused on passage of a national voter registration standard that would have allowed citizens to register to vote on election day (H.R. 5400, H. Rept. 95-318). Although the proposal initially received strong support, negative reactions from local election officials appear to have caused support to erode. The House version never came up for a vote on the floor. Like the House version, the Senate bill (S. 1072, S. Rept. 95-171) was reported out of committee but never came up for a vote. By mid-1977, election-day voter registration was essentially defeated, and there was little or no effort to revive it for the rest of the Carter presidency.

Between 1983 and 1988 various measures to reform voter registration were proposed. Some proposals would have established a national voter registration system based on postcard registration or election-day registration, or both. Some bills proposed providing financial incentives to the states to encourage a more uniform and open registration system. But, while some hearings on voter registration reform were held during the period, no measure ever reached the floor of either the Senate or the House.

While various bills proposing voter registration reform were introduced during the early 1980s, election reform efforts became more narrowly focused. In 1984, Congress passed the Voting Accessibility for the Elderly and Handicapped Act (P.L. 98-435, 98 Stat. 1678). The Act established national requirements for making polling places accessible to the elderly and the handicapped. In addition, the Act required each state to provide "a reasonable number of accessible permanent registration facilities," to "make available registration and voting aids for federal elections for handicapped and elderly individuals," and to require "no notarization or medical certification ... of handicapped voters with respect to an absentee ballot or application for such ballot." The Act was signed into law September 28, 1984.

In 1986, Congress passed and the President signed the Uniformed and Overseas Citizens Absentee Voting Act (P.L. 99-410, 100 Stat. 924). Among other things, the Act required the creation of an official postcard form containing a voter registration and absentee ballot application, required each state to "permit absentee uniformed services voters and overseas voters to use absentee registration procedures and to vote by absentee ballot" in all federal elections, and required states to "permit overseas voters to use federal write-in absentee ballots in general elections for federal office" except when the state provides a state absentee ballot approved by the presidential designee and made available at least 60 days in advance of the election. The Act was signed into law August 28, 1986.[2]

Both P.L. 98-435 and P.L. 99-410 established national voter registration and election standards. Perhaps considered modest by some, these two acts established a much stronger federal presence in state electoral activities than had been the case in the past.

National Voter Registration Reform

Voter turnout in the 1988 presidential election reached its lowest point in 40 years, just slightly more than 50% of the voting-age population. Partly in response to the turnout trends and partly as a continuation of the long-standing efforts by proponents of registration reform, at the beginning of the 101st Congress, several bills were introduced to reform voter registration procedures. For some supporters, these efforts aimed at completing what had been started by the Voting Rights Act of 1965 and its amendments, eliminating the final barriers to voting: voter registration restrictions. For others, the belief that making it easier to register would encourage more voter participation was the driving force behind support for voter registration reform.

The first "motor-voter" bill was introduced by Representatives Swift and Annunzio in the 101st Congress (H.R. 15 and later reintroduced with modifications by Representative Foley as H.R. 2190, H. Rept. 101-243).[3] In the Senate, Senator Ford introduced the companion bill to H.R. 2190, S. 874 (S. Rept. 101-140). In the House, H.R. 2190 received bipartisan support, with Representative Thomas, then ranking member of the Subcommittee on Elections, and Representative Gingrich, then Minority Whip, both sponsors of the bill. H.R. 2190 passed the House February 6, 1990 (vote: 289-132) but was never brought up in the Senate.

S. 250, the National Voter Registration Act of 1991, was introduced in the Senate by Senators Ford and Hatfield in the 102nd Congress. S. 250 differed from the "motor-voter" bill introduced in the 101st Congress (H.R. 2190) and did not receive the same level of bipartisan support. S. 250 passed in the Senate (May 20, 1992, S. Rept. 102-60, vote: 61-38) and in the House (June 16, 1992, vote: 268-153) but was vetoed by President George H. W. Bush.

The provisions of S. 250 were reintroduced at the beginning of the 103rd Congress as H.R. 2 by Representative Swift and as S. 460 by Senator Ford (S. Rept. 103-6). The House passed H.R. 2 on February 4, 1993 (H. Rept. 103-9, vote: 259-160). The Senate passed H.R. 2 with some amendments March 17, 1993, by a vote of 62-37. On May 5, 1993, the House voted on the conference report (Conf. Rept. 103-66, vote: 259-164). The Senate adopted the conference report on May 11, 1993 (vote: 62-36). On May 20, 1993, President Clinton signed the National Voter Registration Act of 1993 into law (P.L. 103-31 [42 U.S.C. § 1973gg et seq.]).

The National Voter Registration Act of 1993: Major Provisions

The National Voter Registration Act of 1993 (NVRA, P.L. 103-31 [42 USC § 1973gg et seq., see http://www.law.cornell.edu/uscode/html/uscode42/usc_sup_01_42_10_20_20_I-H.html]), the so-called "motor-voter" law, required that, for federal elections, states must establish procedures so that eligible citizens may register to vote:

> 1) "by application made simultaneously with an application for a motor vehicle driver's license ... ;
> 2) by mail application ... ; and
> 3) by application in person (A) at the appropriate registration site designated with respect to the residence of the applicant in accordance with state law; and (B) at a federal, state, or nongovernmental office designated under Section 7 (required for state agencies providing public assistance and agencies primarily engaged in providing services to persons with disabilities)." (Sec. 4(a)(1)-(3))

States that had no voter registration requirement (North Dakota) or that allowed citizens to register to vote at polling places on election day, statewide (Minnesota, Wisconsin, and Wyoming), were exempted from the act. This exemption was also applied to New Hampshire and Idaho, which adopted election-day voter registration after the date specified in the original bill language, March 11, 1993. The cut-off date required for state election-day registration was changed (to August 4, 1994) in an amendment contained in P.L. 104-99, passed and signed into law January 26, 1996.

Some suggested that the law would transfer voting registration authority from local election authorities within a state to other state and local agencies. According to proponents, the law required other agencies to make available voter registration forms and materials and to collect completed applications for registering to vote. Only appropriate state election officials, proponents argued, determined whether applications were adequate and, if so, registered the applicants.[4]

With respect to simultaneous application for voter registration and application for a motor vehicle driver's license (the "motor-voter" provision), the law covered new applications, renewals, and changes in address for drivers' licenses. Under the law, an application (or renewal) for a motor vehicle driver's license also served as an application for voter registration, for federal elections, unless the applicant failed to sign the voter registration application (Sec. 5(a)(1)). The voter registration application form was to be a part of the motor vehicle license application form, but would not require any information that duplicated information required in the driver's license portion of the form (Sec. 5(c)(2)). The form could ask for only the minimum amount of information to prevent duplicate registrations and to enable state election officials to determine the eligibility of the applicant and to administer voter registration laws. Further, the law required that the form include a statement that listed each eligibility requirement (including citizenship), contained an attestation that the applicant meet each requirement, and required the signature of the applicant, under penalty of perjury. The form also had to include a statement about penalties for the submission of a false voter registration application and a statement that information about either the declination or the office where the citizen registered would remain confidential. Similar language was required on the mail registration form (Sec. 9(b)). Proponents of P.L. 103-31 considered the "motor-voter" provisions to be the most important of the three procedures. Proponents expected that most voter registration eventually would occur via motor vehicle driver's license applications.[5] Mail and agency registration were included to provide means for persons who did not normally acquire a driver's license.

P.L. 103-31 required the states to accept and use a mail registration application form, as developed by the Federal Election Commission (FEC) (Sec. 6(a)(1)).[6] The mail registration application form, like the motor-vehicle form, could require only such identifying information (including the signature of the applicant) and other information (including data relating to previous registration by the applicant) as was necessary for state election officials to determine the eligibility of the applicant and to administer voter registration laws (Sec. 9(b)(1)). The state was required to make available mail registration forms to governmental and private entities for distribution, emphasizing availability to nongovernmental voter registration programs (Sec. 6(b)). Further, first-time voters who registered by mail might be required to vote in person if the person had not previously voted in that jurisdiction (Sec. 6(c)).

Under the NVRA, all state agencies involved in providing public assistance, as well as all offices in the state providing services to persons with disabilities, were to be designated as voter registration agencies (Sec. 7(a)). The state also was required to designate other offices within the state as voter registration agencies (might include public libraries, schools, offices of city and county governments, fishing and hunting license bureaus, and unemployment compensation offices). These voter registration agencies were required to distribute mail registration application forms to service applicants along with the agencies' own forms, unless the applicants declined to register to vote. The agencies were also to provide assistance in the completion of the mail voter registration application if requested. The agencies were not to attempt to influence applicants to register to vote in a certain way or to discourage the applicants from applying to register to vote. The designated agencies were also required to accept completed voter registration forms for transmittal to the appropriate state election official. Transmittal of completed forms was to occur not later than 10 days after the date of receipt or, if accepted within five days before the end of registration for an election, the application was to be transmitted to an election official not later than five days after receipt (Sec. 7(d)). Also, U.S. armed forces recruitment offices located within the state were designated as voter registration agencies under the NVRA (Sec.7(c)). In 1998, Congress passed and the President signed H.R. 6, the Higher Education Amendments of 1998. The bill, as signed into law, contained a provision that required institutions of higher learning in states covered by the NVRA to make "a good faith effort to distribute a mail voter registration form ... to each student enrolled in a degree or certified program." (See H.R. 6 Sec. 489(b), P.L. 105-244, H.Rept. 105-481, H.Rept. 105-750.)

The NVRA required that, upon receipt and approval or disapproval by the appropriate state election official, each applicant would be sent a notice as to the disposition of the application (Sec. 8(a)(2)). A voter registrant's name was not to be removed from the voter registration list except: at the request of the applicant, by reason of criminal conviction or mental incapacity, by the death of the applicant, or by the applicant moving out of the jurisdiction (Sec. 8(a)(3)-(4)).[7] Registered voters could not be removed from the list for nonvoting (Sec. 8(b)(2)). A state's efforts at maintaining up-to-date voter registration rolls were to be conducted in a "uniform, nondiscriminatory" fashion and had to be in "compliance with the Voting Rights Act of 1965" (Sec. 8(b)(1)). A state could use the U.S. Postal Service's "National Change Of Address" program to help maintain accurate voter registration rolls (Sec. 8(c)(1)). A state could remove a person from its registration list if the registrant notified the election office that he/she had moved or if the registrant failed to respond to a notice sent by the registrar and failed to vote or appear to vote in two federal general elections (Sec. 8(d)(1)). That is, the registrant must respond to the notice within the period covered by two general elections—voting being a means of response.[8]

P.L. 103-31 provided no funding to the states to carry out any of the prescribed features. The states could avail themselves of reduced postal rates for mailing for voter registration purposes (Section 8(h)). However, the U.S. Postal Service has stated that receipt of the reduced postal rates also meant a corresponding reduction in level of service. The FEC was to develop, in cooperation with the states, a mail registration form and to provide reports to Congress every two years on the impact of the act (Sec. 9(a)).[9] Both the attorney general and any aggrieved citizen could seek relief under the act. If, after notification, the appropriate state election official failed to carry out the provisions of the act, an aggrieved citizen might bring a civil suit in a U.S. district court (Sec. 11(a)-(b)). NVRA made a violation of the voter registration procedures as outlined in the law, either by persons or by election officials, a federal offense (Sec. 12). The act went into effect January 1, 1995, or, for states that needed to amend their state constitutions (Arkansas, Vermont and Virginia), January 1, 1996, or 120 days after the amended state constitutions allowed the passage of the supporting legislation, whichever was later.

THE ISSUES, PRO AND CON

Voter Turnout

Many proponents of P.L. 103-31 argued that by making it easier to register eligible citizens, the law would not only increase the number of persons who were registered to vote but also would encourage more voter turnout. They pointed to the fact that usually over 85% of registered citizens vote in general elections, but only about two-thirds of eligible citizens are registered. Proponents marked the fact that over 90% of the voting-age population had a vehicle driver's license or identification card issued by the states. They noted that voter turnout in states that had a form of "motor-voter" registration was higher than in states without "motor-voter" registration. With the simple mechanism of allowing eligible citizens to complete an application to register to vote, proponents argued, the NVRA could easily produce voter registration rates equal to 90% of the voting-age population as compared to the then current registration figures of 65 to 70% of the voting-age population.[10]

Opponents, on the other hand, argued that there was very little evidence that voter turnout would increase even if voter registration increased.[11] They pointed to studies indicating that voter turnout was related to many factors, not just to voter registration procedures. They noted that voter registration reforms in the states had been continuing for many years, that citizens were better educated than in the past, and, still, voter turnout declined.[12] They pointed to almost equal voter turnout in North Dakota and South Dakota in 1992 (67.28% vs. 66.98%, respectively), where North Dakota had no voter registration requirement while South Dakota had one of the stricter registration systems. Since opponents believed that reforming voter registration procedures would lead to only small increases in voter turnout, they described the NVRA as legislation in search of a purpose, with one critic referring to the bill as "auto-fraudo."[13] And after being in effect for 13 years, the statistics indicate that, while voter turnout has increased some, it is still not clear that the act has had a significant impact on voter turnout (see "The Response of the Citizenry" section, below).

Voting Rights

Proponents of the NVRA argued that it was necessary to prevent discriminatory and restrictive procedures that disproportionately affected minorities, the poor, the elderly, and the disabled.

Some of these proponents viewed the NVRA as a necessary extension of the Voting Rights Act of 1965 to eliminate those barriers to voting still experienced by minorities. They argued that each citizen had a right to vote and that voter registration procedures should not be used to test the fortitude and determination of citizens wanting to vote. Although there were legitimate administrative reasons for requiring citizens to register, these proponents argued, the process itself should not discourage citizens from becoming involved in elections. Incorporating voter registration into the drivers' licensing process provided a secure and convenient method for registering voters, proponents contended.[14] Opponents argued, however, that in most states the voter registration procedures were not burdensome and that many states were moving to more efficient and easier systems all the time; 23 states and the District of Columbia already had a form of motor-voter registration prior to the passage of NVRA. Consequently, they claimed, the federal government did not need to pass legislation mandating that each state register voters in the same way. Voter registration administration had traditionally been within the state's purview, opponents stated, and there was little reason to change it.[15]

Costs of Implementation

Opponents argued that the NVRA imposed on the states an expensive, burdensome procedure that was not necessary. For example, 10 states estimated their combined costs for the NVRA would be $87.55 million, and a representative of the California County Clerks' Election Legislation Committee testified that the bill would cost California $26 million per year and the nation between $200 and $250 million per year.[16] Further, opponents noted that the extra time spent in assisting applicants to register to vote in public assistance offices and in offices serving the disabled was likely to mean that fewer of these needy persons would be served adequately.[17]

Proponents argued that the cost figures from states that currently had "motor-voter" registration systems suggested that the costs would be between $0.03 and $0.33 per new registrant.[18] They also pointed out that many estimates used by opponents were based on costs associated with adding the larger number of new registrants, not the costs of implementing "motor-voter." Further, these proponents argued, allowing voter registration to occur over the full election cycle would even out the work of voter registration throughout the period. Also, they noted that the Congressional Budget Office estimated that the proposals (S. 250) would have cost all states between $20 and $25 million a year for the first five years of the program.[19]

Differences between proponents and opponents of the NVRA with respect to cost estimates were likely due more to estimating the costs of two different sets of policies. First, there were the costs of implementing the policies as set out in the NVRA, the costs of registering citizens. Second, there were costs associated with running elections in the states, which might increase because the number of registered voters increased. Costs associated with successfully implementing the voter registration procedures as specified in the NVRA might not be significantly higher than the costs of currently registering citizens in some states except, possibly, for those costs associated with changes to list maintenance. However, if procedures for running elections were directly tied to the number of registered voters, then costs for running an election could have been significantly higher than was currently the case prior to NVRA. If, as proponents argued, the percentage of the voting-age population who were registered increased from 65% to 90%,[20] a change of almost 40%, the impact of the NVRA on running elections might have been significant. However, for whatever reason, this large increase in registered voters has not yet occurred (see below, "The Response of the Citizenry").

Even after 14 years, however, there are few cost estimates for the NVRA. In one of its earlier reports to Congress, the FEC dismissed the idea that a cost estimate was even possible.

> A few people, during the rulemaking process, urged the FEC to collect data regarding the costs of the NVRA. But for several reasons, there is no practical way of determining what the added costs of the NVRA might be ... the FEC would have had to rely on estimated costs. And past experience suggests that estimated costs tend to vary inversely with the estimator's opinion of the law in the first place.... In sum, true cost figures are just too murky.[21]

The report suggests two reasons for the difficulty to develop any cost estimates: (1) the nature of the budgeting process at the local level (most local offices cannot estimate their total election costs much less the costs of a change in voter registration procedures); and, (2) the differential impact of NVRA on the states. Some states already had many of the procedures required while others had none.[22]

The report does go on to point out that the increased mailing costs resulting from the requirements of the NVRA would be what the local election officials would have to bear the most, and this is likely to be substantial. Nationally, this would require:

- quadrennial verification mailings to a minimum of 186,000,000 people
- biennial confirmation mailings to a minimum of 10,000,000 people
- biennial return postage on confirmation postcards from a minimum of 2,000,000 people, and
- biennial acknowledgement mailing to a minimum of 40,000,000 people.[23]

The report notes that the "total postage costs (not to mention printing and handling costs) have now become and will continue to be a major item in every registrar's budget."[24]

U.S. PIRG, a coalition of state public interest research groups (see http://www.uspirg.org/aboutus), recently released a study of 100 counties of various sizes in 36 states that estimated that the cost to conduct registration and run error-correction programs on the voter registration information was $33,467,910 for the 2008 election.[25] According to the report, in counties in the survey with populations under 50,000, total expenditures were estimated at

$86,977 per county; in counties with population between 50,000 and 200,000 persons, the total expenditures were $248,091 per county; and, in counties with total populations between 200,000 and around 1,000,000, the total expenditures per county were estimated to average $1,079,610.[26] As the report notes, these estimates apply only to the 100 counties included in the survey, and were considered to be "conservative."[27]

Some other findings from the report noted that most registrars estimate that their staffs spend at least 50% of their time working on registration issues, while some indicated a greater proportion of time spent on such work. For offices from the small counties (under 50,000 people), the average cost of employee time on registration was estimated to be almost $73,000. For medium-sized counties (50,000-200,000 people), this average cost was estimated to be a little more that $212,000 per office. And for the larger counties (over 200,000 persons), the average cost was estimated to be almost $938,000 for the 2008 election cycle.[28]

Election Fraud

Opponents argued that the NVRA, by making it easier to register to vote and by not providing states with adequate resources to keep their registration lists up-to-date and "clean," opened the door to the possibility of election fraud. And, opponents noted, in those states with large noncitizen populations, the act made it easy for ineligible persons to register to vote. These opponents noted that the process is almost automatic when a person applies for a driver's license, a form of identification that is used by many immigrants to obtain work. The NVRA would be responsible, opponents argued, for the improper voter registration of large numbers of noncitizens.[29]

Proponents argued that P.L. 103-31, by making election fraud a federal offense, strengthened, not weakened, efforts to prevent fraud. Proponents noted that many states with mail registration systems required only an attestation of citizenship or other eligibility requirement and a signature under penalty of perjury, as did the NVRA. Nothing in P.L. 103-31 prevented any state, for example, from asking applicants on the combined form whether or not they were citizens.[30] P.L. 103-31, argued proponents, provided sufficient protection against election fraud.[31] This author was unable to find any systematic evidence or empirical study for or against an increase in voter registration fraud as a result of the implementation of the NVRA, nor have the Federal Election Commission (FEC) or the Election Administration

Commission (EAC) ever mentioned this as a problem that the states have brought up.[32]

NVRA Implementation

The Federal Response

Under the NVRA, no federal agency is responsible for implementation of the act. Although the FEC (EAC) was responsible for developing the mail registration form and for delivering a report to Congress every two years on the effectiveness of the NVRA, it had no further legal authority under the act. Similarly, the Department of Justice could bring suit against a state for the non-implementation of the law, or for violations as specifically outlined in the NVRA, but had no authority to prescribe state implementation of the law. Implementation is, and has always been, the sole responsibility of each state.

Development of the Mail Voter Registration Form

The FEC printed proposed rules relating to the design and content of the NVRA mail registration form in the *Federal Register* on March 10, 1994 (59 F.R. 11211-11222). After extensive discussions with the states covered by the NVRA, the FEC released the final rules relating to the design and content of the mail registration form on June 23, 1994 (59 FR 32311-32325). Final approval of the form was given by the commission on November 8, 1994.

The form required eight data items: (1) full name of applicant; (2) address where applicant lives; (3) mailing address, if different from where applicant lives; (4) month, day, and year of birth; (5) telephone number (optional); (6) voter identification number, if required by state law; (7) political party preference, if required by state law; and (8) race for states required to collect such data under the Voting Rights Act of 1965 (optional for all other states). In addition, certain information had to be included on the form. Among other items were (1) eligibility requirements (including citizenship); (2) an attestation that the applicant met the state's requirements; (3) a signature and date field; (4) a warning about the penalties for submitting false information; (5) a field for the name and address of anyone who helped the applicant to complete the form; (6) a statement that a refusal to register to vote will remain confidential; and (7) a statement that if the applicant does register, the place of registration remains confidential.

As a result of the passage of the Help America Vote Act of 2002 (P.L. 107-252),[33] the following additions were required to be made to the form (see Sec. 303(b)(4)(A)(i-iv)): (1) a question was added specifically asking whether the person registering was a citizen, along with appropriate answer check boxes; (2) a question was added specifically asking whether the person registering to vote was or would be 18 years of age by the next election, again with the appropriate check boxes; (3) a statement was added to the effect that if the person registering to vote had answered "No" to either of the previous questions, then he/she was to stop filling out the form and not register; and (4) a statement was added to the effect that if the completed form was being mailed and the person was registering for the first time, copies of appropriate identification were to be included in the mailing or the person might be required to provide such identification when voting for the first time in the jurisdiction.

Biennial NVRA Report Findings

As a requirement of the NVRA (P.L. 103-31), the FEC (subsequently, the EAC) was responsible for producing a biennial report "assessing the impact of this Act on the administration of elections for federal office ... including recommendations for improvements in Federal and State procedures, forms, and other matters affected by this Act." (Sec. 9(a)(3)) Other than this general mandate, there were no specific instructions about what specific information was to be included in the reports. As a result, the FEC/EAC chose to conduct surveys of the states to collect the information that the FEC/EAC deemed necessary to complete this mandate.[34]

There have been eight such reports.[35] With the exception of the first report, each of the NVRA reports provide detailed discussion and statistics on the voter registration activity of the states for each of the periods under study. These include examinations of total voter registration, new registrants, sources of registrations (i.e., motor-vehicle agencies, mail, in-person at election offices, or other designated state office), and list maintenance issues, including removals from lists and reasons for such removals.

On June 30, 1997, the Federal Election Commission, as part of its obligations under the NVRA, released its second report on the impact of the NVRA. The report was based on the responses of 43 states and the District of Columbia. Six states were not included in the survey because they are exempt from the provisions of the act. Vermont was not included because state constitutional impediments had delayed full implementation. The report found that voter registration (as a percentage of the voting-age population) in states covered by the NVRA rose in 1996 by 1.82 percentage points (or some 3.4 million people) over 1992, the previous comparable election. During the 22 months the act was in effect, a total of almost 41.5 million registration applications or transactions were processed nationwide. Two-thirds, or about 27.5 million, represented new transactions. The duplication rate was 5.2%. The remaining one-third of the total transactions (14 million) represented changes of names and addresses. A total of 8.7 million names were deleted from the registration lists, and another 7.0 million were declared "inactive." In addition, the report noted that voter turnout (as a percentage of the voting-age population) declined by five percentage points as compared to 1992.[36]

The mail registration provisions of the NVRA, according to the FEC report, caused relatively few problems for the states and accounted for nearly one-third of all voter registration applications from 1995 through 1996. The motor vehicle provisions proved easiest for the states to implement and yielded the highest volume of registration applications (33.1% or 13.7 million of all registration applications). Applications received at all designated state voter registration agencies represented over 11% of the total number of registration applications in the United States.[37]

The FEC's report made three recommendations:

1) states, "which do not currently require applicants to provide Social Security numbers", should change election laws to require applicants to provide, at least, the last four digits of their Social Security number and attempt to gather this information for current registered voters;
2) states, which have not yet done so, should "develop and implement a statewide computerized voter registration database", ensuring that "all local registration offices are computerized" and linking their statewide computerized system with the computer systems of other public agencies relevant to the NVRA; and
3) the U.S. Postal Service should create a new class of mail for "official election material," providing the most affordable rates for first class treatment.[38]

The third report of the FEC, covering the period 1997-1998, was released June 30, 1999. The report found that in states covered by the NVRA, active voter registration (as a percentage of the voting-age population) rose 3.72 percentage points, or some 7.1 million people, over comparable figures for 1994. During the period, a total of 35.4 million registration applications or transactions were processed nationwide. About half, or 17.6 million, represented new transactions. The duplication rate was 6.46%. The remaining 43.74% of the total transactions (15.5 million) represented changes of names and addresses. A total of 9.0 million names were deleted from the registration lists, and another 14.6 million were declared "inactive." In addition, the report noted that voter turnout (as a percentage of the voting-age population) declined by 2.38 percentage points as compared to 1994.[39]

Similar to the 1995-1996 period, the 1997-1998 FEC report noted that the mail registration provisions of the NVRA "caused relatively few problems for the states and accounted for nearly one-quarter of all voter registration applications from 1997 through 1998." Likewise, the motor vehicle provisions proved easiest for the states to implement and yielded the highest volume of registration applications (15.2 million, or 42.9% of all registration applications). Voter registration activity by designated state voter registration agencies accounted for 8.22% (2.9 million) of voter registration applications during the period 1997 through 1998. The FEC made the same three recommendations that it had made in the second report.[40]

The fourth report of the FEC, covering the period 1999-2000, released June 30, 2001, was based on the survey responses from the 44 states and the District of Columbia covered by the NVRA. The report found that in states covered by the NVRA active voter registration (as a percentage of the voting-age population) rose slightly by 0.35 percentage points over comparable figures for 1996 (73.45% to 73.80% of the voting-age population). However, active voter registration nationally (includes the states not covered by the NVRA) declined slightly from 72.77% in 1996 to 72.63% in 2000. During the period, a total of 45.7 million registration applications or transactions were processed nationwide. About half, or 22.5 million, represented new transactions. The duplication rate was 7.72% (3.5 million). The remaining 43.04% of the total transactions (19.7 million) represented changes of names and addresses. A total of 13.0 million names were deleted from the registration lists, and another 18.3 million were declared "inactive."[41]

Similar to the two earlier periods, the FEC report noted that the mail registration provisions of the NVRA caused relatively few problems for the states and accounted for nearly one-third of all voter registration applications (14.2 million). The registration application via motor vehicle offices again yielded the highest volume of registration applications (17.4 million, or 38.1% of all registration applications). However, survey results indicated "numerous problems with completed voter registration applications being forwarded from motor vehicle offices to the appropriate election official in a timely manner during the most recent election cycle." Voter registration at designated state voter registration agencies accounted for 7.58% (3.5 million) of voter registration applications.[42]

The FEC again made the same three recommendations that it had made in the two previous reports. The report also added four other recommendations based specifically on the experiences of the 2000 election. These were the following:

1) "that states develop and implement an on-going, periodic training program for relevant motor vehicle and agency personnel regarding their duties and responsibilities under the NVRA as implemented by the state's law;"
2) "that states require motor vehicle and agency offices to promptly transmit information regarding voter registration applicants electronically to the appropriate election office with documentation to follow;"
3) "that states devise a procedure whereby voters may cast a provisional ballot at the polls on election day under circumstances prescribed in state law but at least for the purposes of the fail-safe provisions of the NVRA;" and,
4) "that states adopt the practice of mailing a forwardable notice to all persons who are removed from the voter registration list whose mail has not previously been returned as undeliverable."[43]

The fifth report of the FEC, covering the period 2001-2002, released June 30, 2003, was based on the survey responses from the 44 states and the District of Columbia covered by the NVRA. The report found that in states covered by the NVRA voter registration (as a percentage of the voting-age population) declined slightly by 1.54 percentage points from comparable figures for the last mid-term election in 1998 (71.55% to 70.01% of the voting-age population). During the period, a total of 37.5 million registration applications or transactions were processed nationwide. Over half or 19.7 million represented new transactions. The duplication rate was 8.74%. The remaining 38.68% of the total transactions represented changes of names and addresses. A total of 15.0 million names were deleted from the registration lists, and another 20.6 million were declared "inactive."[44]

Similar to the earlier periods, the FEC report noted that the mail registration provisions of the NVRA caused relatively few problems for the states and accounted for more than one-fourth of all voter registration applications (27.64%). The registration application via motor vehicle offices again yielded the highest volume of registration applications (42.77% of all registration applications received). Unlike the previous reporting period, survey results indicated a significant decrease in the number of problems reported in the state motor vehicle registration programs, although timeliness in transmitting voter registration application remained a problem.[45] Voter registration at designated state voter registration agencies accounted for 5.83% of voter registration applications.[46]

NVRA Reports two through four, as discussed above, all made the same three core recommendations: (1) states should amend their election laws to use the last four digits of the social security number for all new voter registration applications; (2) states should develop and implement a statewide voter registration database, linking all local offices to a centralized database; and, (3) the United States Postal Service should create a new class of mail for "official election materials" with favorable rates and first class treatments.[47] In addition, NVRA Report 1999-2000 had added four other recommendations: (1) states should develop and implement an on-going, periodic training program for relevant motor vehicle and agency personnel regarding their duties with respect to NVRA; (2) states should require motor vehicle and agency offices to promptly transmit information regarding voter registration applicants electronically to the appropriate election officials; (3) states should develop a procedure for provisional voting, extending or helping to implement better the fail-safe procedures in NVRA; and, (4) states should adopt the procedure of mailing a forwardable notice to all persons removed from voter registration lists.[48] With the exception of the recommendation relating to a special mailing category for NVRA election materials and training programs for state motor vehicle and agency personnel, all of the other FEC recommendations were incorporated, as a whole or in part, in the Help America Vote Act of 2002 (P.L. 107-252). Consequently, the 2001-2002 NVRA Report only repeated the recommendation about the special mailing category and urged the states to set up training programs for state motor vehicle and agency personnel.[49]

The sixth report, and the first report submitted by the newly created EAC, covered the period 2003-2004 and was released June 30, 2003. It was based on the survey responses from the 48 states, the District of Columbia, and three of the four territories (American Samoa, Puerto Rico, and the U.S. Virgin Islands). The report found voter registration (as a percentage of the voting-age population) declined slightly by 0.4 percentage points from comparable figures for the last presidential election in 2000 (78.9% to 78.5% of the voting-age population). During the period, a total of 49.6 million registration applications or transactions were processed nationwide. Over half (26 million) represented new transactions. Nearly 3.5 million (7.3%) were duplication registrations.

About 1.6 million applications (5.2%) were rejected or determined to be invalid. Some 15.2 million of the total transactions represented changes of names and addresses. Nearly 12.6 million names were deleted from the registration lists, while another 10.7 million were declared "inactive."[50]

The EAC report noted that the mail registration accounted for almost one-third of all voter registration applications (32.4%). The registration applications received via motor vehicle offices yielded the highest volume of registration applications, but only 32.8% of all registration applications received. The number of registration applications received in person at election or registrar offices amounted to 25.4% of all registration applications. Almost 11% of all registration applications came from designated state voter registration agencies.[51]

The recommendations of the EAC in the sixth report more closely reflected the passage of HAVA's provisions relating to the requirement that each state must establish a statewide voter registration database by January 1, 2006 (P.L. 107-252, Sec. 303(a)(1)(A)) than any provisions specific to NVRA. First, states should provide for electronic transmission of voter registration information from state motor vehicle and other designated NVRA state voter registration agencies directly to local election officials. Second, "states should perform list maintenance through electronic coordination with state and federal databases." The report specifically mentioned the U.S. Postal Service National Change of Address and Social Security Death Index databases, as well as records from U.S. Attorneys and U.S. District Courts concerning criminal conviction records. And third, "states should develop statewide voter registration databases that are capable of tracking a registrant's voting and registration history."[52]

The seventh report covered the period 2005-2006 and was released June 30, 2007. It was based on the survey responses from all states, the District of Columbia, and four territories (American Samoa, Guam, Puerto Rico, and the U.S. Virgin Islands). The report found voter registration (as a percentage of the voting-age population) increased by 1.9 percentage points over comparable figures for the last mid-term election in 2002 (74.7% to 76.6% of the voting-age population). During the period, a total of 36.3 million registration applications or transactions were processed nationwide. Nearly half (17.3 million) represented new transactions. Nearly 2.2 million were duplication registrations. Some 10.9 million of the total transactions represented changes of names and addresses. Nearly 13 million names were deleted from the registration lists, while another 9 million were declared "inactive."[53]

The EAC report noted that the mail registration accounted for almost a quarter of all voter registration applications (22.8%). The registration applications received via motor vehicle offices yielded the highest volume of registration applications (45.7% of all registration applications received). The number of registration applications received in person at election or registrar offices amounted to 19.8% of all registration applications. Over 11% of all registration applications came from designated state voter registration agencies.[54]

For the seventh report EAC merged two recommendations and kept one recommendation from its sixth report, as well as added two additional recommendations. The first recommendation merges the first and second recommendations from the 2003-2004 Report and reads, "states should continue to improve and modernize their electronic reporting and list maintenance systems." The second recommendation repeats recommendation three from the 2003-2004 Report. The third recommendation in the 2005-2006 report is a message to the states about standardizing the information needed for the NVRA report to Congress, which reads as follows:

> states should set up their statewide data collection system to facilitate the collection and reporting of information mandated by NVRA. States should work in partnership with the EAC to establish agreed-upon standards for the handling of active and inactive voters, overseas and military voters, and other important categories for the NVRA.

The fourth recommendation in this report is similar to a previous recommendation in the NVRA Report 2001-2002, and reads "states should provide training to all agencies involved in voter registration."[55]

The eighth and most recent EAC report covered the period 2007-2008, and was released June 30, 2009. It was based on survey responses from all states, the District of Columbia, and four territories (America Samoa, Guam, Puerto Rico, and the U.S. Virgin Islands). The report found voter registration (as a percentage of the voting-age population) increased by 1.8 percentage points over comparable figures for the last Presidential election cycle (2003-2004, from 79.7% to 81.7% of the voting-age population).[56] During the period covered by the report, a total of more than 60 million registration applications or transactions were processed nationwide. Of these, 24.6 million (or over 40%) represented new voters, which was 7.3 million more new voters than had registered in the prior election cycle (2005-2006).[57] More than 20 million of these registration forms requested a change to name, address, or party of the registrant.[58] About 3.6 million applications were determined to be duplicates and another 1.7 million were determined to be invalid or otherwise rejected. Combined, duplicates and invalid registration applications constituted 8.8% of the registration applications for this period. More than 12 million names were deleted from the registration lists, "for reasons including death, felony conviction, failure to vote in consecutive elections, having moved from one jurisdiction to another, or at the voter's request."[59]

The EAC report noted that mail registration accounted for 28.8% of all applications. Registration applications received via motor vehicle offices yielded the highest volume of registration applications, although only slightly above mail registration (30.1% of all registration applications received). The number of registration applications received in person or at election or registrar offices amounted to 14.9% of all registration applications.[60] Over 6% (3,807,991) of all registration applications came from designated state voter registration agencies and 1.1% came through internet applications.[61]

The EAC's eighth report retained one recommendation from its previous report and added five new recommendations. The retained recommendation reads, "states should continue to improve and modernize their electronic reporting and list maintenance systems." Second, the EAC recommends that the "states should explore supporting a coordinated data collection effort that allows local jurisdictions to provide election data to their State election offices." Third, the EAC recommends that "states should provide EAC with information on their proven best practice models of election data collection in order to facilitate sharing with all States through EAC's clearinghouse function." Fourth, the EAC recommends that "states are encouraged to use technology to ease the workload on their election offices, as they deem appropriate." Fifth, the EAC recommends that "states should encourage their public service agencies to remind voters to check and update their registration information." And sixth, the EAC recommends that "for the purpose of compiling comparable election data from future EAC Election Administration and Voting Surveys EAC will continue to work towards a common understanding of election terms."[62]

Department of Justice Activity

As of May 1994, 23 states had complied with the NVRA, according to a Department of Justice news release (Alaska, Arkansas, Arizona, Colorado, Connecticut, Delaware, Florida, Georgia, Hawaii, Iowa, Kentucky, Maine, Maryland, Massachusetts, Mississippi, Missouri, Nebraska, Oregon, South Dakota, Tennessee, Utah, Washington, and West Virginia). At that time,

Justice officials indicated that enforcement of the NVRA would be one of the Department's highest priorities.

On January 22, 1995, the Justice Department filed suit against California, Illinois, and Pennsylvania for failure to implement the NVRA by January 1, 1995. South Carolina was also sued on February 6, 1995. Subsequently, on May 4, 1995, the Justice Department and Pennsylvania agreed that the state would fully implement the NVRA, pending passage of legislation. Both California and Illinois, after having decisions handed down by the respective U.S. Courts of Appeal that ruled against their challenges, implemented NVRA. Also, on April 25, 1995, the Justice Department notified Montana about its failure to implement parts of the NVRA (the state failed to implement agency-based registration and to bring its mail registration form into line with the NVRA requirements). In a reply letter dated May 4, Montana agreed to correct the oversight. Although Georgia and Texas developed the NVRA proposals and had implemented the NVRA voter registration procedures, the Justice Department challenged aspects of the implementations under provisions of the Voting Rights Act of 1965. Subsequently, these were resolved and both remain in compliance. Differences that the Justice Department had with Louisiana's implementation plan also were resolved, and Louisiana reached full compliance.

During the period 1998-2009, the Justice Department filed suit in five cases brought against three states (New York, Indiana, and Missouri) for failure to implement parts of the NVRA. The three New York cases concerned the designation of state voter registration agencies.[63] Both the Indiana case[64] and the Missouri case[65] concerned the obligations of the state for list maintenance and whether or not the states were in compliance. The remaining suits filed during this period relating to the enforcement or lack of enforcement of the provisions of NVRA (86 cases[66]) were brought by private persons or organizations. For whatever reason, the Justice Department brought very few suits against the states during this period. Arguably, this was due to the perception that states' enforcement of the provisions of NVRA was adequate, to a lack of resources at the Department for such activities, to a policy decision not to exert much effort behind such enforcement, or to a combination of the three.

Recently, there has been criticism of the Justice Department, mainly directed toward the operations under the Bush Administration with respect to enforcement of NVRA. Most of this criticism has been directed at the lack of enforcement of provisions relating to NVRA's agency-based voter registration provisions. An article by Michael Slater, deputy director of Project Vote, appeared in The League of Women's Voters online publication, *The National Voter* (see http://www.lwv.org/AM/Template.cfm?Section= Home& Template=/TaggedPage/TaggedPageDisplay.cfm&TPLID=19&ContentID= 10530), February 2008 edition. In the article, Slater discussed the issue and provided statistics suggesting the lack of state efforts in promoting agency-based voter registration. Slater also argued that "the U.S. Department of Justice has failed to investigate recent allegations that states are not complying with the public agency requirements of the NVRA"[67] However, as noted above, the NVRA reports indicate that, while there was a drop in applications in state voter registration agencies during the period 1997-2002, states reported the same level of applications received from these agencies in the 2003-2004 and 2005-2006 periods as they had received in the 1995-1996 reporting periods. However, the level of applications dropped by almost half from the state agencies during the 2007-2008 reporting cycle[68]

More recently, the Chairman of the Senate Rules and Administration Committee, Senator Charles Schumer, in hearings in early April 2009, pressed Attorney General Eric Holder to "pull out all the stops" and sue any state not complying with the agency-based provisions of the NVRA. In a statement, Senator Schumer noted that "this law is supposed to simplify the voter registration process, but it has been complicated by the rogue behavior of a large batch of states."[69] There is some evidence that even before the criticisms, the Department of Justice had made moves to enforce these provisions of the NVRA.[70]

The Response of the States

Overall, response from most states was cooperative and, despite misgivings about the costs, aimed at the implementation of the NVRA by the January 1, 1995, deadline. However, a few states decided to avoid or challenge the NVRA.

As explained earlier, the provisions of the NVRA were not applicable to states that had had no voter registration system on or before March 11, 1993 (North Dakota), that had had an election-day voter registration procedure at every polling place in effect on or before March 11, 1993 (Minnesota and Wisconsin), or had made the adoption of an election-day registration system contingent on the passage of the NVRA (Wyoming). In an attempt to avoid the implementation of the provisions of the NVRA, which were viewed as costly, Idaho, in January 1994, and New Hampshire, in March 1994, passed legislation adopting election-day voter registration and made it retroactive as of March 11, 1993. Congress effectively ratified this strategy when, in an amendment contained in P.L. 104-99 (signed January 26, 1996), it amended the designated date as specified in the NVRA from March 11, 1993, to August 4, 1994.

Mississippi passed legislation giving state and local officials the authority to implement the NVRA, but only for federal elections. The state legislature established a dual registration system, providing that citizens who wished to cast a ballot in state and local elections had to register separately in accordance with prior registration law. On April 20, 1995, four citizens (later joined by the U.S. Department of Justice) sued over the dual registration requirements, charging that they violated the Voting Rights Act of 1965, as amended. On March 31, 1997, the Supreme Court ruled unanimously that Mississippi had violated the pre-clearance provisions of the Voting Rights Act when it chose to establish a dual voter registration system by applying the provisions of the NVRA solely to elections for federal office without first submitting the electoral changes for Justice Department approval. Mississippi had argued that, as it made no changes to state law, it did not need to seek pre-clearance for the new system, having already received clearance for its implementation plan of the NVRA provisions. As a result of the decision, Mississippi was required to submit its current dual registration system for approval by the Justice Department.[71] On October 5, 1998, a three- judge federal panel ordered Mississippi to allow all persons who registered under the NVRA provisions to vote in state and local elections until Mississippi enacted a law implementing the NVRA that was pre-cleared by the Justice Department. Subsequently (in 2000), Mississippi laws were brought into compliance.

After the first two years (1995-1996) of implementation, litigation, and an election, state and local officials appeared to come to terms with the NVRA. However, proposals were suggested to amend the NVRA to make it easier to administer and prevent election fraud. Some proposals suggested would (1) require a Social Security number on voter registration applications; (2) change the citizenship attestation to a question ["Are you a citizen?" YES NO] where applicants would have to say yes to be eligible to register; (3) eliminate the NVRA-mandated second mailings to persons already identified by the Postal Service as having moved; and (4) enact legislation to help reduce the costs of NVRA-mandated mailings.[72] Election officials formed a task force, the Joint Election Officials Liaison Committee (JEOLC) to negotiate and lobby for various changes in the law, as well as to work with the U.S. Postal Service to devise procedures that would make it easier for election offices to comply with some provisions of the NVRA. The JEOLC was composed of representatives from the International Association of Clerks, Recorders, Election Officials, and Treasurers (IACREOT), the National Association of County Recorders and Clerks (NACRC), the National Association of State Election Directors (NASED), and the Election Center.

A survey conducted by the National Association of Secretaries of State (NASS) of 43 states covered by the NVRA indicated that gains in voter registration had occurred in every state. Of the 43 states, 41 reported drivers' license bureaus effective in registering voters, and 35 indicated that other agencies also proved effective. More than half of the states indicated that their biggest problem was transmittal difficulties involving untimely, incomplete, unsigned, and illegible registration forms. About half thought that the NVRA restrictions on removing voters from the rolls contributed significantly to the greater number of registrants. However, other states applauded the NVRA for helping them maintain accurate registration lists.[73]

The Response of the Citizenry

Based on the most recent NVRA Report, voter registration (as a percentage of the voting-age population) in those states covered by the NVRA (45 states) was 71.67% in 1992, 68.32% in 1994, 75.58% in 1996 (the first federal election after implementation), 75.97% in 1998, 76.72% in 2000, 74.19% in 2002, 78.37% in 2004, 76.31% in 2006, and 81.61% in 2008.[74] Thus, comparing the difference in mid-term elections, voter registration increased almost eight percentage points (7.99%) between the pre-NVRA, 1994 mid-term election and the 2006 midterm election. Similarly, comparing the difference in presidential elections, voter registration increased almost ten percentage points (9.55%) between the pre-NVRA 1992 presidential election and the 2008 presidential election. The bulk of the change came immediately following the implementation of the NVRA.

As noted earlier, many proponents appeared to believe that the NVRA would not only increase voter registration but would also increase voter participation. Comparing post-NVRA voter turnout to the 1992 presidential election voter turnout might be somewhat misleading, as that election included a popular third-party candidate. Voter turnout (as a percentage of the voting-age population) in presidential elections since 1980 was the following: 1980—52.56%, 1984— 53.11%, 1988—50.11%, 1992—55.09%, 1996—

49.77%, 2000—51.12%, 2004 — 55.4%, 2008—56.9%.[75] In other words, voter turnout in the United States has fluctuated between a low of less than 50% in 1996 to a high of 55% in 2004, and almost 57% in 2008. With the low and high turnout coming in the post-NVRA period, it is not clear whether NVRA has had an impact on voter turnout in presidential elections. Voter turnout in off-presidential election years was the following: 1982—40.52%, 1986—36.40%, 1990—36.52%, 1994—38.78%, 1998—36.15%, 200 —36.3%, and 2006—37.1%.[76] Mid-term elections have not shown much fluctuation since 1986, and while there was a drop in turnout in the single post-NVRA election, 1994 was the year that both the Senate and the House of Representatives turned Republican. All-in-all, while the NVRA has been in effect for 14 years, there appears to be little evidence that the NVRA has had a major impact on voter turnout.

THE CONGRESSIONAL RESPONSE POST-NVRA

The NVRA was not supported by most Republicans in the 103rd Congress, and a similar bill had been vetoed by President Bush in 1992. With the ascendancy of the Republican Party in the 104th Congress, and given the criticism of the NVRA as an "unfunded mandate" of the federal government by several prominent Republican governors from large states,[77] attempts to repeal or modify the NVRA appeared certain. However, while the Republican Party controlled both the House and Senate, its control in the Senate would not have prevented Democratic Senators from mounting a filibuster against proposals to change the NVRA. Further, with the White House in the hands of a Democrat (President Clinton) who supported the NVRA, any changes in the NVRA that were not bipartisan would almost certainly have been vetoed.

In the 105th Congress, as in the 104th, bills were introduced to repeal the NVRA (H.R. 345), to make the provisions voluntary (H.R. 2115), and to modify the provisions in some fashion. The modifications proposed consisted of the following: (1) requiring citizens to produce a Social Security number in order to register to vote (H.R. 224, H.R. 2076, and S. 1561); (2) requiring proof of citizenship in order to register to vote (H.R. 1139, H.R. 2076, and S. 1561); (3) allowing states to require photographic identification in order to cast a ballot (H.R. 1139 and S. 1561); (4) repealing the mail voter registration provisions of NVRA (H.R. 2076 and S. 1561); (5) changing purge rules in the NVRA to make it easier and less expensive for states to purge their voter registration rolls of ineligible persons (H.R. 224, H.R. 2076, H.R. 3485, and S. 1561); and, (6) making optional for the states the requirement to allow registrants who change their address to vote at the polling place for their old address, the "failsafe voting" provision (H.R. 2076 and S. 1561).

In addition, Representative Horn introduced legislation that would have required the Immigration and Naturalization Service (INS) and the Social Security Administration, at the request of federal, state, or local election officials, to provide information on the citizenship status of persons attempting to register to vote (H.R. 1428).

The House Oversight Committee (renamed the Committee on House Administration in the 106th Congress) held hearings on H.R. 224, H.R. 1139, H.R. 1428, and H.R. 2076 on November 6, 1997.[78] On February 12, 1998, H.R. 1428 was brought up for a vote under suspension of the rules in the House of Representatives, a procedure that requires a two-thirds majority to pass, and was defeated (vote: 210-200).

On March 18, 1998, Representative Thomas, then chairman of the Committee on House Oversight, introduced legislation (H.R. 3485) that, in part, would have established a pilot project in five states (California, New York, Texas, Florida, and Illinois) of the program proposed in H.R. 1428. H.R. 3485 was reported out of the Committee on House Oversight on March 23, 1998 (H.Rept. 105-457). On March 30, 1998, H.R. 3581, a revision of H.R. 3485, was introduced and brought up for a vote in the House, under suspended rules, and was defeated (vote: 74-337).

On May 6, 1998, the House passed (414-4) the Higher Education Amendments of 1998, H.R. 6, which contained an amendment offered by Representative Clayton (H.Amdt. 583), requiring institutions of higher learning to distribute the NVRA mail voter registration application form to each student during enrollment, unless the student, in writing, declined such a form. The Senate version of H.R. 6 passed without this provision. In conference, the amendment was modified to require institutions in states covered by the NVRA to make "a good faith effort to distribute a mail voter registration form ... to each student enrolled in a degree or certified program." In addition, the revised language required the institutions to request voter registration forms from the state 120 days prior to the deadline for registering to vote, but it allowed an institution to implement its own program without interference from state officials. The conference report (H.Rept. 105-750) passed the House by voice vote September 28 and passed the Senate (vote: 96-0) September 29. The legislation was signed by President Clinton (P.L. 105-244) October 7, 1998.

As the 106th Congress began, two voter registration related bills were introduced in the House. On January 6, 1999, Representative Stump, as he did in the 105th Congress, introduced a bill (H.R. 38) to repeal the NVRA. On the same day, Representative McCollum introduced H.R. 180, a duplicate of the bill he introduced in the 105th Congress (H.R. 224). In May, Senator Warner introduced legislation to deal with campaign finance reform (S. 1107S. 1107, essentially a duplicate of S. 1561, introduced in the 105th Congress, see above). This bill amended parts of the NVRA by (1) repealing the mail voter registration requirements, (2) requiring states to obtain an applicant's Social Security number when attempting to register to vote, (3) requiring applicant's registering at a state motor vehicle office to submit proof of citizenship, (4) allowing states to purge names from voter registration lists because the registrants had failed to vote for period of time after the registrant was notified, and (5) repealing the limited provisional voting provisions of the NVRA. In September, 1999, Representative Luther introduced legislation to amend the NVRA by requiring states to provide citizens the right to register at the polling place on election day (H.R. 2864). There was no action on any of these bills in the 106th Congress.

In reaction to the events of the 2000 Presidential election, a number of bills were introduced in the 107th Congress to reform the election administration process. While some of these bills focused solely on voter registration (H.R. 128, H.R. 189, H.R. 829, H.R. 2687, S. 2226), much of the effort was focused on a more comprehensive response. The efforts culminated in the passage of the Help America Vote Act of 2002 (HAVA) (P.L. 107-252).[79] HAVA addressed voter registration in four areas:

1) it created the Election Assistance Commission (EAC) and transferred FEC's responsibilities with respect to NVRA to EAC (Sec. 201, see http://www.law.cornell.edu/uscode/42/usc_sec_42_00015321----000-.html; 202, see http://www.law.cornell.edu/uscode/42/usc_sec_42_00015322----000-.html; 209, see http://www.law.cornell.edu/uscode/42/usc_sec_42_00015329----000-.html; 803, see http://www.law.cornell.edu/uscode/42/usc_sec_42_00015532----000-.html), specifically with respect to the development and maintenance of the federal mail voter registration form (Sec. 303(b)(4), see http://www.law.cornell.edu/uscode/42/usc_sec_42_00015483----000-.html) and the biennial reports on the impact of the NVRA;

2) it specified that each state "shall implement, in a uniform and nondiscriminatory manner, a single, uniform, official, centralized, interactive computerized statewide voter registration list defined, maintained, and administered at the State level that contains the name and registration information of every legally registered voter in the State and assigns a unique identifier to each legally registered voter in the State" (Sec. 303(a)(1)(A), see http://www.law.cornell.edu/uscode/42/ usc_sec_42_00015483----000-.html) and "perform list maintenance with respect to the computerized list on a regular basis" in accordance with the provisions of NVRA (Sec. 303(a)(2), see http://www.law.cornell.edu/uscode/42/usc_sec_42_00015483----000-.html);
3) it required the use of the driver's license number or the last four digits of the social security number of the applicant on all voter registration applications (Sec. 303(a)(5)(A), see http://www.law.cornell.edu/uscode/42/usc_sec_42_00015483----000-.html), as well as requiring that the Social Security Administration develop relationships with the departments of motor vehicles in each state to assist in list verification (Sec. 303(a)(5)(B), see http://www.law.cornell.edu/uscode/42/usc_sec_42_00015483----000-.html); and,
4) it expanded the "fail safe voting"[80] provisions of NVRA to provisional voting (Sec. 303(a)(5)(A)-(B), see http://www.law.cornell.edu/uscode/42/usc_sec_42_00015482----000-.html).

In the 108th Congress, legislation was introduced to repeal NVRA (H.R. 2139), to require proof of citizenship to register to vote (H.R. 4174, H.R. 4530), to standardize the treatment of ex-felons with respect to their right to register to vote (H.R. 1433, H.R. 4578), to require states "to provide notice and an opportunity for review prior to removing any individual from the official list of eligible voters by reason of criminal conviction or mental incapacity" (H.R. 4250), to require same-day or election-day voter registration (H.R. 1510, H.R. 3153), and to allow pre-registration to individuals to register to vote prior to meeting the age requirement (H.R. 4972). None of the bills reached beyond the committee assignment.

In the 109th Congress, legislation was introduced to require states to institute same-day or election-day voter registration (H.R. 496, H.R. 533, H.R. 939, H.R. 3557, S. 17. S. 450), to require proof of citizenship when registering

(H.R. 4989), to require a photo-identification when registering to vote (H.R. 2250), to allow removal from registration lists for failure to vote (H.R. 2778), to prohibit removal from voter registration lists due to correctable errors and removal for felony conviction or death unless the comparison database meet standards set by the Director of the National Institute of Standards and Technology (H.R. 3094), to delay the implementation of the state voter registration database requirement in HAVA for four years (H.R. 3163), to require states to keep the name and addresses of victims of domestic violence that appeared on state voter registration databases confidential (H.R. 4462), and to require states to produce durable voter registration cards (H.R. 4989). One other bill, S. 414, had several goals. It would have required the use of the Social Security number in registering voters, required that all states synchronize all state voter registration databases, eliminated third party voter registration, modified conditions for removal of names from voter registration databases, and clarified procedures for first-time registrants. None of the bills reached the floor of the House or the Senate.

The legislative activity in the 110th Congress, in many ways, reproduced that in the 109th. Same-day or election-day voter registration was introduced in a variety of bills (H.R. 2457, H.R. 5628, H.R. 1381, H.R. 5946, S. 730, S. 804, S. 2959). Three bills contained provisions aimed at requiring notice before any names could be removed from voter registration lists (H.R. 7244, S. 730, S. 804). Legislation also was introduced to control whom and how voter registration forms were distributed (H.R. 301), to require the acceptance of any type of voter registration form sent by overseas military or civilians (S. 3073), to require the acceptance of a newly created official federal voter registration and ballot application from overseas citizens (H.R. 4237), to make institutions of higher education state voter registration agencies as specified in NVRA (S. 3390, H.R. 6704), to require the addition of a statement on voter registration application forms that stated that any alien who used the form to register was deportable under the Immigration and Nationality Act (H.R. 5695), to prohibit states from not accepting voter registration forms from third parties (S. 1487), to require photographic identification to register to vote (H.R. 879), to promote pre-registration for students under 18 (S. 3100), and to have the EAC study Internet voter registration (S. 730, S. 804). The only legislation that passed the House, however, was a bill that required the Department of Veterans Affairs to designate all of its public facilities as state voter registration agencies as defined under NVRA (H.R. 6625). This bill was not acted upon in the Senate.

Based on the legislative agenda thus far in the 111th Congress, the areas of concern with respect to voter registration have not changed from previous legislative sessions. H.R. 105 has been introduced; it requires same-day voter registration for all states, notice of removal of names from voter registration lists, and a requirement that states develop an internet voter registration application procedures. H.R. 1719 also requires that the states provide internet voter registration application procedures. Two bills propose to make institutions of higher learning state voter registration agencies as specified in the NVRA (H.R. 1729, S. 1125). H.R. 1739 focuses on making it easier for overseas military and civilians to register and vote absentee by creating a new combined official federal voter registration and absentee ballot application form and requiring all states to accept the forms. S. 1103 establishes standards for how voter registration forms can be distributed.

CONCLUDING OBSERVATIONS

The National Voter Registration Act of 1993 has been the law of the land for 16 years and has been in effect for 14 years. The courts have resolved many of the initial issues. A review of the FEC reports appears to indicate that the states have come to terms with the provisions, despite the fact that state election officials advocate that the federal government should provide funding for the implementation of aspects of the act.

There may still be some problems with implementation at the local levels and with the training of nonelection officials who are responsible under the NVRA for providing voter registration services. As noted above, some opponents would like to curtail parts of the NVRA; proponents, however, do not think the NVRA has gone far enough. Some are calling for voter registration reform that would include what has been called "universal voter registration," where the government is responsible for registering all citizens to vote unlike the system used in the United States that relies on individuals to register themselves.[81] Others have suggested minor changes in NVRA, like making it "opt-out" instead of "opt-in" (i.e., automatic registration when an applicant receives a driver's license or benefits at designated state voter registration agencies, unless specifically deciding to "opt-out"), but with more enforcement of the provisions that are currently in place.[82] How and whether the Congress decides to respond to these calls for reform remains to be seen.

End Notes

[1] U.S. Congress, Senate Committee on Rules and Administration, *Voter Registration: Assessing Current Problems*, 111th Cong., 1st sess., March 11, 2009, http://rules.senate.gov/public/index.cfm?FuseAction=CommitteeSchedule.Hearing&Hearing_id=c33b5ae8-aee8-413e-85 db-a256ce6169f6; Tamar Lewin, "Voter Registration by Students Raises Cloud of Consequences," New York Times, September 8, 2008, p. A13, http://www.nytimes.com/2008/09/08/education

[2] CRS Report RS20764, *The Uniformed and Overseas Citizens Absentee Voting Act: Overview and Issues*, coordinated y Kevin J. Coleman.

[3] U.S. Congress, House Committee on House Administration, *Voter Registration*, hearings on H.R. 15, H.R. 17 and H.R. 87, 101st Cong., 1st sess., March 21, 1989 (Washington: GPO, 1989).

[4] U.S. Congress, Senate Committee on Rules and Administration, *National Voter Registration Act of 1993*, report to accompany S. 460, 103rd Cong., 1st sess., S. Rept. 103-6, (Washington: GPO, 1993), p. 7.

[5] Ibid., p. 5

[6] Subsequently delegated to the Election Assistance Commission (EAC) when FEC functions were transferred because of HAVA in 2002 (P.L. 107-252, title VIII, Sec. 802(a), Oct. 29, 2002, 116 Stat. 1726., U.S.C. 42 § 15532).

[7] These provisions were strengthened somewhat by HAVA, P.L. 107-252 (42 U.S.C., § 15483 (2)(A), see http://www.law.cornell.edu/uscode/html/uscode42/usc_sec_42_00015483----000-.html) by requiring that the new required statewide voter registration database be compared to other appropriate statewide databases.

[8] The provision about "failure to vote in two consecutive elections" was clarified in HAVA, P.L. 107-252 (42 U.S.C. § 15483 (4), see http://www.law.cornell.edu/uscode/html/uscode42/usc_sec_42_00015483----000-.html).

[9] Again, these functions were transferred to the EAC by HAVA, P.L. 107-252, see footnote 6.

[10] U.S. Congress, Senate Committee on Rules and Administration, *National Voter Registration Act of 1993*, report to accompany S. 460, 103rd Cong., 1st sess., S. Rept. 103-6, (Washington: GPO, 1993), p. 5.

[11] Ibid., pp. 51-52.

[12] For a different view of "decreasing voter turnout," see Michael P. McDonald and Samuel Popkin, "The Myth of the Vanishing Voter," *American Political Science Review*, vol. 94, no. 4 (2001), pp. 963-974.

[13] Sen. Mitch McConnell, "National Voter Registration Act of 1992," remarks in the Senate, daily edition, vol. 138, Sept. 21, 1992, p. S14206.

[14] Ibid., pp. 2-3. Also see U.S. Congress, House Committee on House Administration, *National Voter Registration Act of 1993*, report to accompany H.R. 2, 103rd Cong., 1st sess., H. Rept. 103-9 (Washington: GPO, 1993), pp. 2-5.

[15] S. Rept. 103-6, pp. 50-51.

[16] Ibid., p. 51. H. Rept. 103-9, p. 36.

[17] Sen. Mitch McConnell, "National Voter Registration Act of 1992," remarks in the Senate, daily edition, vol. 138, Sept. 21, 1992, p. S14206.

[18] Sen. Daniel K. Akaka, "National Voter Registration Act of 1993," remarks in the Senate, *Congressional Record*, vol. 139, Mar. 17, 1993, p. S3002.

[19] S. Rept. 103-6, p. 41.

[20] S. Rept. 103-6, pp. 2, 5.

[21] The Federal Election Commission, *The Impact of the National Voter Registration Act of 1993 on the Administration of Elections for Federal Office 1995-1996*, Washington, DC, June 30, 1997, http://www.eac.gov/files/clearinghouse/reports_surveys/ The%20Impact%20of%20the%20NVRA%20of%201993%20on%20Admin%20of%20Elections%20for%2097-98.pdf, p.14.

[22] Ibid., p. 14.

[23] Ibid., p. 15. These are the figures for the 1995-1996 period. Comparable figures given for the 2001-2002 period were 160,000,000, 20,000,000, 4,000,000, and 37,000,000, respectively. See, the 2001-2002 NVRA Report, The Federal Election Commission, *The Impact of the National Voter Registration Act of 1993 on the Administration of Elections for Federal Office 2001-2002*, Washington, DC, June 30, 2003, p. 24., http://www.eac.gov/files/clearinghouse/reports_surveys/ The%20Impact%20of%20the% 20NVRA%20of%201993%20on%20Admin%20of%20Elections%20for%2099-00.pdf

[24] NVRA Report 1995-1996, p. 15.

[25] Lisa Gilbert, *Saving Dollars, Saving Democracy: Cost Savings for Local Election Officials through Voter Registration Modernization*, U.S. PIRG, May 2009, p. 3, http://www.uspirg.org/home/reports/voting—civic-participation/voting—civic-participation/saving-dollars-saving-democracy—cost-savings-for-local-elections-officials-through-voter-registration-modernization.

[26] Ibid., p. 3.

[27] Ibid., pp. 3-4, 20.

[28] Ibid., p.20.

[29] S. Rept. 103-6, pp. 52-57. H. Rept. 103-9, pp. 34-37.

[30] HAVA requires that language to this effect be included in the mail registration form developed by the Election Assistance Commission (EAC).(U.S.C. 42 § 15483(b)(4)(A)(i)).

[31] S. Rept. 103-6, pp. 5, 11-13, 20-21, 37. H. Rept. 103-9, pp. 10-11, 14, 20-21.

[32] See also, Barry H. Weinberg, *The Resolution of Election Disputes: Legal Principles That Control Election Challenges, 2nd Edition* (Washington, DC: International Foundation for Electoral Systems, 2008), pp. 85-101.

[33] For a full discussion of the Help America Vote Act, see CRS Report RL32685, *Election Reform: The Help America Vote Act and Issues for Congress*, by Eric A. Fischer and Kevin J. Coleman.

[34] For a clear description of how the FEC determined its reporting requirements and, thus the reporting requirements of the states, see Federal Election Commission, *The Impact of the National Voter Registration Act of 1993 on the Administration of Elections for Federal Office 1995-1996*, Washington, DC, June 30, 1997, http://www.eac.gov/files/clearinghouse/ reports_surveys/ The%20Impact%20of%20the%20NVRA%20of% 201993 %20on%20Admin%20of%20Elections%20for%2095-96.pdf. Henceforth, NVRA Report 1995-1996.

[35] NVRA Report 1995-1996; Federal Election Commission, The Impact of the National Voter Registration Act of 1993 on the Administration of Elections for Federal Office 1997-1998, Washington, DC, June 30, 1999, henceforth known as NVRA Report 1997-1998, http://www.eac.gov/files/clearinghouse/reports_surveys/ The%20Impact%20of%20the%20NVRA%20of%201993%20on%20Admin%20of%20Elections%20for%2097-98.pdf; Federal Election Commission, The Impact of the National Voter Registration Act of 1993 on the Administration of Elections for Federal Office, 1999-2000, Washington, DC, June 30, 2001, henceforth, known as NVRA Report 1999- 2000, http://www.eac.gov/files/clearinghouse/reports_surveys/

The%20Impact%20of%20the%20NVRA%20of%201993%20on%20Admin%20of%20Elections%20for%2099-00.pdf; Federal Election Commission, The Impact of the National Voter Registration Act of 1993 on the Administration of Elections for Federal Office 2001-2002, Washington, DC, June 30, 2003, henceforth, known as NVRA Report 2001- 2002, http://www.eac.gov/files/clearinghouse/reports_surveys/ The%20Impact%20of%20the%20NVRA%20of%201993%20on%20Admin%20of%20 Elections%20 for%2099- 00.pdf; Elections Assistance Commission, The Impact of the National Voter Registration Act of 1993 on the Administration of Elections for Federal Office 2003-2004, Washington, DC, June 30, 2005, henceforth, known as NVRA Report 2003-2004, http://www.eac.gov/program-areas/research-resources-and-reports/copy_of_ docs/reportsand-surveys-nvra-2004-survey-htm.pdf/attachment_download/file; Elections Assistance Office, The Impact of the National Voter Registration Act of 1993 on the Administration of Elections for Federal Office 2005-2006, Washington, DC, June 30, 2007, henceforth known as NVRA Report 2005-2006, http://www.eac.gov/program-areas/ researchresources-and-reports/copy_of_docs/the-impact-of-the-national-voter-registration-act-on-federal-elections-2005-2006/ attachment_download/file; Elections Assistance Office, The Impact of the National Voter Registration Act of 1993 on the Administration of Elections for Federal Office 2007-2008, Washington, DC, June 30, 2009, henceforth known as NVRA Report 2007-2008, http://www.eac.gov/program-areas/research-resources-and-reports/completed-research-and-reports/program-areas/research-resources-and-reports/copy_of_docs/nvra-report-final_congress

[36] NVRA Report 1995-1996, p. 1.

[37] NVRA Report 1995-1996, pp. 1-2.

[38] NVRA Report 1995-1996, pp. 2-3.

[39] NVRA Report 1997-1998, p. 1.

[40] NVRA Report 1997-1998, pp. 1-2.

[41] NVRA Report 1999-2000, p. 1.

[42] NVRA Report 1999-2000, pp. 1-2.

[43] NVRA Report 1999-2000, pp. 3-4.

[44] NVRA Report 2001-2002, p. 1.

[45] NVRA Report 2001-2002, pp. 1-2.

[46] NVRA Report 2001-2002, p. 14.

[47] See NVRA Report 1995-1996, pp. 37-43, NVRA Report 1997-1998, pp. 21-26, NVRA Report 1999-2000, pp. 29- 35. Also, on May 4, 1995, in testimony before the Senate Subcommittee on Treasury, Postal Service, and General Government of the Senate Appropriations Committee, Postmaster General Marvin Runyon noted that the NVRA cost the agency $2.1 million dollars that year and described it as an "unfunded mandate" for the Postal Service. Under the NVRA, the Postal Service is required to provide the states with "third-class" rates, available to nonprofit organizations, for voter registration mailings. However, several states have complained that it is almost impossible to comply with certain provisions of the NVRA relating to voter list maintenance because the Postal Service does not, under nonprofit mailing rates, normally return nonforwardable mailings to the sender. Nonforwardable mailings can be used as a first step in determining if a citizen has moved from an old address under the NVRA.

[48] NVRA Report 1999-2000, pp. 35-37.

[49] NVRA Report 2001-2002, p. 3.

[50] NVRA Report 2003-2004, p. 1-2, 9-12.

[51] NVRA Report 2003-2004, pp. 9-12.

[52] NVRA Report 2003-2004, pp. 13-14.
[53] NVRA Report 2005-2006, p. 1.
[54] NVRA Report 2005-2006, pp. 1-2.
[55] NVRA Report 2005-2006, pp. 13-14.
[56] NVRA Report 2007-2008, p. 29.
[57] NVRA Report 2007-2008, p. 1.
[58] NVRA Report 2007-2008, p. 1.
[59] NVRA Report 2007-2008, pp. 1-2.
[60] NVRA Report 2007-2008, p. 1.
[61] NVRA Report 2007-2008, p. 39.
[62] NVRA Report 2007-2008, pp. 8-9.
[63] *U.S. v. New York*, 3 F. Supp. 2d 298 (E.D. NY); *U.S v. New York*, 255 F. Supp. 2c 73 (E.D. NY); 2007 U.S. Dist. LEXIS 21722.
[64] 2006 U.S. Dist. LEXIS 45640.
[65] 2006 U.S. Dist. LEXIS 32499.
[66] Based on a LEXIS search covering the period, searching for the "National Voter Registration Act."
[67] Michael Slater, "Compliance with the NVRA: Not Optional," *The National Voter*, February 2008, pp. 11-12.
[68] Applications received from state voter registration agencies in the 1995-1996 period constituted 11% of all applications received. The same was true in the 2003-2004 period and the 2005-2006 periods, see NVRA Report, 1995- 1996, pp. 1-2; NVRA Report 2003-2004, pp. 9-12; NVRA Report 2005-2006, pp. 1-2. However, during the 2007-2008 period this percentage dropped to 6.3%, see NVRA Report 2007-2009, p. 39.
[69] See Jordy Yager, "Schumer Wants States Sued Over Voter Registration," http://thehill.com/leading-the-news/ schumer-wants-states-sued-over-voter-registration-2009-04-07.html. Also, see Sen. Schumer's website at http://schumer.senate.gov/new_ website/record.cfm?id=311271. Also, Senator Charles Schumer, "Schumer Urges DOJ: Sue States That Flout Voter Registration Law," press release, April 7, 2009, http://schumer. senate.gov/new_website/ record.cfm?id=311271.
[70] See, "Project Vote Applauds Justice Department Enforcement of NVRA in Illinois," http://www.reuters.com/article/ pressRelease/idUS53510+20-Dec-2008+PRN20081220.
[71] *Young et al. v. Fordice et al.* 520 U.S. 273 (1997), see http://www.law.cornell.edu/ supct/html/95-2031.ZS.html.
[72] Richard G. Smolka, "Election Officials Liaison Group Advised of Legislative Opportunities, Postal Rate Increase," in *Election Administration Reports*, vol. 27 (Washington: Jan. 13, 1997), pp. 2-4; Richard G. Smolka, "JEOLC Hears Congressional Staff Outline Plans for Legislation," in *Election Administration Reports*, vol. 28 (Washington: Jan. 19, 1998), p. 5.
[73] Richard G. Smolka, "NASS Survey Identifies Gains and Some Problems with NVRA," in *Election Administration Reports*, vol. 27 (Washington: Feb. 13, 1997), pp. 1-3.
[74] NVRA Report 2005-2006, Table 1a. Registration History, p. 18 and NVRA Report 2007-2008, Table 1a. Registration History, p. 15. The percentages are based on the figures in the column labeled "Reported Registration." Empty cells were completed by values from an earlier CRS Report, CRS Report 96-932, *Voter Registration and Turnout: 1948-1994*, by Royce Crocker (archived; available from the author). The table was then recomputed by the author. A full copy of the table is available on request.
[75] CRS Report 96-932, *Voter Registration and Turnout: 1948-1994*, by Royce Crocker (archived; available from the author); CRS general distribution memorandum, *Voter Registration and*

Turnout: 1996 (Washington: Dec. 30, 1997), p.1. The 2004 and 2008 figures comes from Michael P. McDonald, *United States Election Project*," 2004 General Election Turnout Rates", http://elections.gmu.edu/Turnout_2004G.html and 2008 General Election Turnout Rates", http://elections.gmu.edu/Turnout_2008G.html. It should be noted that McDonald does not recommend using the Voting-age population as the divisor for computing turnout, preferring his Voter Eligible Population. This is, without question a better measure, especially when making comparisons between states and countries. However, for historical consistency with the figures used by the FEC(EAC), the author chose to use figures based on the voting-age population. For the same period, McDonald's figures based on his Voter Eligible Population are 1980—54.2%, 1984—55.2%, 1988—52.8%, 1992—58.1%, 1996—51.7%, 2000—54.2%, 2004—60.1%, and 2008—61.7%.

[76] Ibid., p. 10, for 1982-1994. Unpublished CRS data for 1998. Also for 2002 and 2006, see McDonald, http://elections.gmu.edu/Turnout_2002G.html, and http://elections.gmu.edu/Turnout_2006G.html. McDonald's figures for the mid-term elections based on his Voter Eligible Population divisor are 1982 — 42.1%, 1986 — 38.1%, 1990 — 38.4%, 1994 — 41.1%, 1998 — 38.1%, 2002 — 39.5%, 2006 — 40.3%.

[77] Alan Greenblat, "Court Rejects 'Motor Voter' Case, But the Battle Isn't Over," Congressional Quarterly, weekly report, vol. 54 (Washington: Jan. 27, 1996), p. 232.

[78] U.S. Congress, House Committee on House Oversight, Campaign Reform: Ballot Integrity/Disclosure, hearings on H.R. 224, H.R. 345, H.R. 1139, H.R. 1428, H.R. 2076, and H.R. 2115, 105th Cong., 1st sess., Nov. 6, 1997 (unpublished).

[79] For an overview of the provisions of P.L. 107-252, see CRS Report RL32685, *Election Reform: The Help America Vote Act and Issues for Congress*, by Eric A. Fischer and Kevin J. Coleman. Also see the committee report, U.S. Congress, House Committee on House Administration, *Help America Vote Act of 2002*, committee print, 107th Cong., 2nd sess., October 8, 2002, 107-730 (Washington: GPO, 2002).

[81] Wendy Weiser, Michael Waldman, and Renee Paradis, *Voter Registration Modernization*, Brennan Center for Justice, New York University School of Law, New York, NY, 2009, http://www.brennancenter.org/content/resource/universal_voter_registration_draft_summary/; FairVote, "Universal Voter Registration, http://www.fairvote.org/?page= 65; Progressive States Network, "Universal Voter Registration: A New Initiative to Increase Electoral Participation and Reduce Voter Suppression, http://www.progressivestates.org/ node/22476.

[82] Common Cause, "Voter Registration," http://www.commoncause.org/site/pp.asp?c =dkLNK1MQIwG&b=4923169.

[80] Fail safe voting essentially allowed a voter who had moved within the voting jurisdiction to vote in either his new or old poll place and to alter the information on his/her voter registration record at the polling place. See P.L. 103-31, Sec. 8(e).

In: Voting and Election Reform
Editor: Nicole P. Fletcher

ISBN: 978-1-61324-640-5

Chapter 4

CONGRESSIONAL AUTHORITY TO STANDARDIZE NATIONAL ELECTION PROCEDURES*

Kenneth R. Thomas

SUMMARY

Events surrounding the 2000 presidential election have led to increased scrutiny of voting procedures in the United States, including efforts to establish national standards for issues such as the administration of voter registration, balloting, tabulating, and reporting election results. This report focuses on the constitutional authority and limitations relevant to Congress standardizing these and other election procedures.

Congress's authority to regulate a particular election may vary depending on whether that election is for the Presidency, the House, the Senate, or for state and local positions. Further, there may be variation in whether a particular aspect of elections, such as balloting procedures, is amenable to regulation. Consequently, evaluating the authority to establish uniform election procedures would appear to require an examination of a variety of different proposals and scenarios.

Although the Constitution is silent on various aspects of the voting process, it seems to anticipate that states would be primarily responsible for establishing election procedures. Federal authority to regulate federal

* This is an edited, reformatted and augmented version of a Congressional Research Services publication, CRS Report for Congress RL 30747, from www.crs.gov, dated April 23, 2009.

elections, however, is also specifically provided for in the Constitution. There are two main provisions at issue—Article I, §4, cl. 1, which provides Congress the authority to set the "Times, Places and Manner" of congressional elections, and Article II, §1, cl. 4, which provides that Congress may designate the "Time" for the choosing of Presidential Electors.

Congress's power is broadest in the case of House elections, which have historically always been decided by a system of popular voting. Congressional power over Senate elections, while almost as broad as it is for House elections, contains one exception—that Congress may not regulate "the Places of chusing Senators." The power of Congress to regulate presidential elections, is not, as clearly established as the power over House and Senate elections. As noted above, the text of the Constitution provides the Congress only the limited power to designate the "Time" of the choosing of Presidential Electors. It does appear that Congress's regulatory authority over presidential elections is more extensive than might appear based on the text of Article II, §1, cl. 4.The case law on the extent of this power is, however, ambiguous.

The Constitution does not grant Congress general legislative authority to regulate the manner and procedures used for elections at the state and local level. Congress, however, does have authority under the Civil War Amendments, and the 19th, 24th, and the 26th Amendments to prevent discrimination in access to voting; and it has exercised that power extensively to regulate state and local elections, as well as federal elections. Congress also has expansive authority to spend money for the general welfare, and allocation of certain grant monies can be conditioned on compliance by state or local officials with national standards for election procedures.

It should be noted that legislation in this area may require state agencies to comply with federal election mandates. The Constitution, however, contemplates that states will bear the burden of administering federal elections subject to federal regulation. Thus, such mandates do not appear to run afoul of the "anti-commandeering" requirements of the Tenth Amendment. To the extent that there are gaps in Congress's power to regulate federal, state, or local elections, however, Congress might use the Spending Clause to condition the receipt of federal monies upon compliance with federal requirements.

BACKGROUND

Events surrounding the 2000 presidential election led to an increased scrutiny of current voting procedures in the United States. For instance, efforts have been made to establish national standards for the administration of voter registration, balloting, tabulating, or reporting election results. This report focuses on the constitutional authority and limitations that are relevant to Congress's standardizing these and other procedures.

In evaluating any such proposals, an initial question to be asked is which elections will be affected. Traditionally, all voting, whether federal, state or local, occurs in local precinct polling places; and state or local authorities have a significant role in regulating such voting. Congress, however, also has authority to regulate elections, and that authority may vary depending on whether the election is for the Presidency, the House, the Senate, or for state or local offices. Further, there may be variation in whether a particular aspect of an election, such as balloting procedures, is amenable to congressional regulation. Consequently, the authority for Congress to establish standardized election procedures would appear to require an evaluation of a variety of different proposals and scenarios.

In 2002, in response to the 2000 presidential election, Congress passed the Help America Vote Act of 2002 (HAVA).[1] HAVA provides federal requirements for several aspects of election administration, including voting systems, provisional ballots, voter information, voter registration, and the provision of identification by certain voters. For instance, HAVA requires that voting systems used in federal elections provide for error correction by voters (either directly or via voter education and instruction), manual auditing for the voting system, accessibility to disabled persons (at least one fully accessible machine per polling place) and alternative languages, and a method to meet federal machine error-rate standards.[2] Systems are also required to maintain voter privacy and ballot confidentiality, and states are required to adopt uniform standards for what constitutes a vote on each system.[3]

HAVA also provides extensive regulation of the manner in which states maintain voter registration lists.[4] Under these provisions, a chief state election official must create a uniform centralized, computerized statewide-voter registration list, which must be coordinated with other agency databases within the state. The state election system must include systems to ensure that voter registration records in the state are accurate and are updated regularly. HAVA also requires that the chief state election official and the official responsible for the state motor vehicle authority enter into an agreement to match information in the database of the statewide voter registration system with information in the database of the motor vehicle authority to verify the accuracy of the information provided on applications for voter registration.

Various proposals have been made regarding further standardizing of election procedures, including:

- Requiring state agencies to share information to facilitate accurate registration lists
- Standardizing mail-in and absentee balloting
- Establishing a uniform closing time for polls
- Establishing multiple day elections
- Standardizing the number and accessibility of polling stations
- Regulating supervision of voting
- Standardization of vote counting, compilation, and publication of results
- Allocating electoral votes within state based on popular votes.

RELEVANT CONSTITUTIONAL PROVISIONS

The authority of Congress to legislate regarding these various issues in different types of elections would appear to derive principally from two constitutional provisions.

Article I, §4, cl. 1

> The Times, Places and Manner of holding Elections for Senators and Representatives, shall be prescribed in each State by the Legislature thereof; but the Congress may at any time by Law make or alter such Regulations, except as to the Places of chusing Senators.

Article II, §1, cl. 4

> The Congress may determine the Time of chusing the [Presidential] Electors, and the Day on which they shall give their votes; which Day shall be the same throughout the United States.

HOUSE ELECTIONS

Although the Constitution is silent on various aspects of the voting process, the Constitution seems to anticipate that states would be primarily responsible for establishing election procedures for congressional elections. Federal authority to regulate congressional elections is specifically provided for in the Constitution. This power is at its most broad in the case of House elections, which have historically always been decided by a system of popular voting.[5] As noted above, Article I, §4, cl. 1 states that Congress may determine "the Times, Places and Manner" for such elections. The Supreme Court and lower courts have interpreted the above language to mean that Congress has extensive power to regulate most elements of a congressional election.

For instance, the Supreme Court has noted that the right to vote for Members of Congress is derived from the Constitution and that Congress therefore may legislate broadly under this provision to protect the integrity of this right.[6] The Court has stated that the authority to regulate the "times, places and manner" of federal elections:

> embrace[s] [the] authority to provide a complete code for congressional elections, not only as to times and places, but in relation to notices, registration, supervision of voting, protection of voters, prevention of fraud and corrupt practices, counting of votes, duties of inspectors and canvassers, and making and publication of election returns; in short, to enact the numerous requirements as to procedure and safeguards which experience shows are necessary in order to enforce the fundamental right involved.... [Congress] has a general supervisory power over the whole subject.[7]

Consequently, it would appear that Congress would have broad authority to implement the various proposals listed above as regards House elections.

SENATE ELECTIONS

Unlike House elections, Senate elections were, until ratification of the 17th Amendment, decided not by popular vote, but by a vote of the state legislatures. This helps explain why congressional power over Senate elections, while almost as broad as it is for House elections, contains one exception—that Congress may not regulate "the Places of chusing Senators." As originally drafted, this language would have limited the authority of Congress to designate where state legislatures would meet for such votes. This deference to the prerogatives of state legislatures would appear to be obsolete now that all Senate elections are decided by popular vote. However, nothing in the 17th Amendment explicitly repealed this restriction, and the meaning of the clause could apply to congressional regulation of establishment of the sites for popular voting.

Arguably, if Congress attempted to establish legislation regulating where states must establish polling sites for Senate elections, such legislation might run afoul of this provision. On the other hand, for practical purposes, most states, if subjected to federal regulation for House elections establishing the location of polling place, would be likely to follow such directions for Senate elections occurring at the same time, if no other reason than administrative convenience.

PRESIDENTIAL ELECTIONS

The power of Congress to regulate presidential elections is not as clearly established as the power over House and Senate elections. First, the text of the Constitution provides a more limited power to Congress in these situations. Whereas Article I, §4, cl. 1 allows regulation of the "time, place and manner" of congressional elections, Article II, §1, cl. 4 provides only that Congress may determine the "time" of choosing presidential electors. Further, despite modern state practice providing for popular voting for electors, the appointment of presidential electors was historically and remains today a power of the state legislatures.[8] Consequently, principles of federalism might incline the Supreme Court to find the appointment of presidential electors less amenable to federal regulation. The exception to this would be congressional authority under the Civil War Amendments (13th, 14th, and 15th); these powers are addressed in the following section on regulating state and local elections.

The case law on this issue is ambiguous, although Congress's regulatory authority over presidential elections does seem to be more extensive than it might appear based on the text of the Constitution. For instance, the Court has allowed congressional regulation of political committees which seek to influence presidential elections, arguing that such legislation is justified by the need to preserve the integrity of such elections. In *Burroughs v. United States*,[9] the Supreme Court reasoned that:

> [w]hile presidential electors are not officers or agents of the federal government, they exercise federal functions under, and discharge duties in virtue of authority conferred by, the Constitution of the United States. The President is vested with the executive power of the nation. The importance of his election and the vital character of its relationship to and effect upon the welfare and safety of the whole people cannot be too strongly stated. To say that Congress is without power to pass appropriate legislation to safeguard such an election from the improper use of money

> to influence the result is to deny to the nation in a vital particular the power of self protection. Congress, undoubtedly, possesses that power, as it possesses every other power essential to preserve the departments and institutions of the general government from impairment or destruction, whether threatened by force or by corruption.[10]

A question arises, however, whether *Burroughs*, which involves the regulation of third parties to elections, can be distinguished from the regulation of states directly regarding their administration of presidential elections. In *Burroughs*, the Court distinguished the legislation under consideration (regulation of political committees) from legislation more directly dealing with state appointment of electors, noting that:

> The congressional act under review seeks to preserve the purity of presidential and vice presidential elections. Neither in purpose nor in effect does it interfere with the power of a state to appoint electors or the manner in which their appointment shall be made. It deals with political committees organized for the purpose of influencing elections in two or more states, and with branches or subsidiaries of national committees, and excludes from its operation state or local committees. Its operation, therefore, is confined to situations which, if not beyond the power of the state to deal with at all, are beyond its power to deal with adequately. It in no sense invades any exclusive state power.[11]

Under this language, procedures within the province of states, such as the allocation of electors by a state, would appear to fall outside of the doctrine established in *Burroughs*. Although the Court was not asked to evaluate whether Congress had the power to establish the manner in which the presidential electors were appointed, the language above would appear to indicate that the Court in *Burroughs* had not intended its decision to extend Congress's authority to regulate presidential elections so that it was coextensive with the power to regulate congressional elections.

Surprisingly, however, three United States Courts of Appeal, relying on *Burroughs,* reached precisely the opposite result. In upholding the validity of congressional regulation of registration procedures for federal elections under the National Voter Registration Act of 1993 (Motor Voter Act),[12] three federal circuits appeared to find that Congress had the same authority to regulate presidential elections as it did House and Senate elections.[13] However, of the three opinions, two made only passing references to the issue, and only the Seventh Circuit discussed it at any length.

In *ACORN v. Edgar*, Chief Judge Posner of the Seventh Circuit wrote that:

> Article I, §4 [providing authority over congressional elections] ... makes no reference to the election of the President, which is by the electoral college rather than by the voters at the general election; general elections for President were not contemplated in 1787.... But these turn out not to be [a] serious omission[] so far as teasing out the modern meaning of Article I, §4 is concerned. Article II provides [congressional authority over the Time of choosing Electors.] Article II, §1 ... has been interpreted to grant Congress power over Presidential elections coextensive with that which Article I ,§4 grants it over congressional elections.
>
> *Burroughs v. United States,* 290 U.S. 534 (1995).[14]

It should be noted that the federal registration standards developed under Motor Voter could probably have been decided under Congress's power over congressional elections, so that the reasoning of these cases would not appear essential to their holdings. These broad holdings, however, do stand as some of the few modern interpretations of Article II, §1, cl. 4 and *Burroughs*.[15] Those cases' interpretations, however, would appear to be at odds with the limiting language of *Burroughs* quoted previously.[16]

Resolution of this issue may ultimately be important to any determination of whether proposals to standardize election procedures could be specifically applied to presidential elections. Where congressional and presidential election procedures are likely to overlap, such as requirements for absentee balloting, uniform closing times, multiple day elections, number and accessibility of polling stations, *etc*., regulation of congressional elections may be for practical purposes sufficient. However, where the issue at hand is unique to presidential elections (e.g., allocation of electors based on popular vote), the resolution of this issue may become essential.

STATE AND LOCAL ELECTIONS

Congress does not have general legislative authority to regulate the manner and procedures used for elections at the state and local level. Congress, however, does have extensive authority under the Civil War Amendments,[17] the 19th Amendment,[18] the 24th Amendment,[19] and the 26th Amendment[20] to prevent discrimination in access to voting, and it has exercised that power extensively over state and local, as well as federal, elections.[21] Thus, to the extent that national ballot standards could be established as a means to avoid disenfranchisement, regulation of state and local elections could be established.

Such power does, however, have limits. For instance, the Fourteenth Amendment provides that states shall not deprive citizens of "life, liberty or property" without due process of law nor deprive them of equal protection of the laws, and section 5 of that Amendment provides that Congress has the power to legislate to enforce its provisions. Thus, in *Katzenbach v. Morgan*,[22] the Court held that §5 of the Fourteenth Amendment authorized Congress not just to enforce the provisions of the Fourteenth Amendment as defined by the courts, but to help define its scope. In *Katzenbach*, the Court upheld a portion of the Voting Rights Act of 1965 which barred the application of English literacy requirements to persons who had reached sixth grade in a Puerto Rican school taught in Spanish.

In *Flores v. City of Boerne,*[23] however, the Court limited the reach of this authority. In *Flores*, the Court struck down the Religious Freedom Restoration Act (RFRA)[24] as beyond the authority of Congress under §5 of the Fourteenth Amendment. RFRA, passed in response to the 1990 Supreme Court case of *Oregon v. Smith*,[25] was an attempt by Congress to reinstate the compelling governmental interest test which had been used to challenge the application of generally applicable laws to religious institutions.

The *Flores* case arose when the City of Boerne denied a church a building permit to expand, because the church was in a designated historical district. The church challenged this action, asserting that the city had not demonstrated a compelling interest in applying its zoning legislation to the church as required by RFRA. In striking down RFRA, the Supreme Court held that there must be a "congruence and proportionality" between the injury to be remedied and the law adopted to that end. RFRA focused on no one area of alleged harm to religion, but rather broadly inhibited the application of all types of state and local regulations to religious institutions. Since the Court found no pattern of the use of neutral laws of general applicability to disguise religious bigotry and animus against religion, it found RFRA to be an overbroad response to a relatively nonexistent problem.

Similarly, it might be difficult to justify an overall regulation of state and local elections based on the Fourteenth Amendment, absent a strong showing of systemic disenfranchisement of voters. Rather, *Flores* would seem to dictate that Congress would need to establish narrow proposals showing that particular voting procedures threatened constitutional rights, and that the legislation was a congruent and proportional response to such threat.

For instance, the question has been raised as to whether the case of *Bush v. Gore,*[26] which found Equal Protection concerns regarding the disparate treatment of voters, would support congressional legislation to standardize voting technologies and procedures. A close examination of that case, however, would seem to indicate that the Supreme Court did not intend to significantly extend the application of the Equal Protection Clause, and consequently the Court may not be amenable to the expansion of congressional authority in this area.

In *Bush v. Gore*, a dispute arose regarding, among other things, how to count punch-card election ballots where the paper "chads" had not been fully dislodged. The Supreme Court held that the failure of the Florida Supreme Court to set standards for evaluating these ballots violated the Equal Protection Clause of the 14th Amendment. On its face, this would appear to make it more likely that Congress could pass legislation under §5 of the 14th Amendment to avoid these or similar problems. Under the previously discussed case law, such laws would be valid if Congress could establish that disparity in the use of voting technologies and procedures has historically resulted in violations of the Equal Protection Clause.[27]

In fact, it would be likely that Congress could establish a record of disparity in the application of voting technologies and procedures, as states have historically delegated authority over elections to lesser subdivisions such as electoral districts. These subdivisions, in turn, choose voting methods and procedures appropriate to their size, density and budget, with only general guidance from the state legislatures. Thus, significant variations in voting technologies and procedures probably do occur in most states. There is language in *Bush v. Gore,* however, which would make it unlikely that such variations would be found to be a violation of the Equal Protection Clause. In essence, this language appears to limit the holding in *Bush v. Gore* to only those election procedures that are under the control of a judicial officer.

> The recount process, in its features described here, is inconsistent with the minimum procedures necessary to protect the fundamental right of each voter in the special instance of a statewide recount under the authority of a single state judicial officer. Our consideration is limited to the present circumstance, for the problem of equal protection in election processes generally presents many complexities.... The question before the Court is not whether local entities, in the exercise of their expertise, may develop different systems for implementing elections. Instead, we are presented with a situation where a state court with the power to assure uniformity has ordered a statewide recount with minimal procedural

> safeguards. When a court orders a statewide remedy, there must be at least some assurance that the rudimentary requirements of equal treatment and fundamental fairness be satisfied.

Based on the above language, disparity in voting procedures is only likely to rise to the level of constitutional violation when such disparate procedures are under the authority of single judicial officer, such as during a recount. It is not clear that Congress could establish a history of voting discrimination in these circumstances. Nor is it likely that the Court would find significant intrusions on state or local election district authority to set technology or procedure standards to be proportionate and congruent to such violations as have existed. Consequently, it would appear that the impact of the case of *Bush v. Gore* on the issue of congressional authority over elections would be minimal.

TENTH AMENDMENT

The Tenth Amendment provides that "powers not delegated to the United States by the Constitution, nor prohibited by it to the States, are reserved to the States respectively, or to the people." While this language would appear to represent one of the most clear examples of a federalist principle in the Constitution, it has not had a significant impact in limiting federal powers. Initially, the Supreme Court interpreted the Tenth Amendment to have substantive content, so that certain "core" state functions would be beyond the authority of the federal government to regulate. Thus, in *National League of Cities v. Usery*,[28] the Court struck down federal wage and price controls on state employees as involving the regulation of core state functions.[29] The Court, however, overruled *National League of Cities* in *Garcia v. San Antonio Metropolitan Transit Authority*.[30] In sum, the Court in *Garcia* seems to have said that most disputes over the effects on state sovereignty of federal commerce power legislation are to be considered political questions, and that the states should look for relief from federal regulation through the political process.[31] This appeared to have ended the Court's attempt to substantively limit federal government regulation of the states.

The Court soon turned, however, to the question of how the Constitution limits the process by which the federal government regulates the states. In *New York v. United States*,[32] Congress had attempted to regulate in the area of low-level radioactive waste. In a 1985 statute, Congress provided that states must either develop legislation on how to dispose of all low-level radioactive waste generated within the state, or the state would be forced to take title to such waste, which would mean that it became the state's responsibility. The Court found that although Congress had the authority under the Commerce Clause to regulate low-level radioactive waste, it had only the power to regulate the waste directly. Here, Congress had attempted to require the states to perform the regulation, and decreed that the failure to do so would require the state to deal with the financial consequences of owning large quantities of radioactive waste. In effect, Congress sought to "commandeer" the legislative process of the states. In the *New York* case, the Court found that this power was not found in the text or structure of the Constitution, and it was thus a violation of the Tenth Amendment.

A later case presented the question of the extent to which Congress could regulate through a state's executive branch officers. This case, *Printz v. United States*,[33] involved the Brady Handgun Act. The Brady Handgun Act required state and local law-enforcement officers to conduct background checks on prospective handgun purchasers within five business days of an attempted purchase. This portion of the act was challenged under the Tenth Amendment, under the theory that Congress was without authority to "commandeer" state executive branch officials. After a historical study of federal commandeering of state officials, the Court concluded that commandeering of state executive branch officials was, like commandeering of the legislature, outside of Congress's power, and consequently a violation of the Tenth Amendment.

Although there do not appear to have been any Tenth Amendment challenges to HAVA, there have been challenges to the Motor Voter Act[34] (discussed previously). As noted above, Congress has the authority under Article I, § 4 to provide for the "The Times, Places and Manner of holding Elections for Senators and Representatives." The term "Manner" of holding elections has been held to include state systems for registering voters.[35] The "Motor Voter" Act, for instance, provides that a state driver's license application contain information enabling it to also serve as an application to register to vote in federal elections. The act also requires states to create a mail-order form for registering to vote, and that states designate all offices that dispense welfare or provide benefits to the disabled as voter registration agencies. In addition, the law requires that states assist voting by persons in certain vulnerable populations.

The provisions of the "Motor Voter" Act have been found to fall within the power of Congress.[36] In *ACORN v. Edgar*,[37] the Seventh Circuit observed that the language of Article I, § 4 "is broadly worded and has been broadly interpreted." The court noted that the phrase "Manner" of holding elections has even been interpreted to extend beyond general federal elections to include the regulation of primaries.[38] Further, the court noted that such authority as is found in Article I, § 4 is supplemented by the Necessary and Proper Clause.[39]

One might ask whether the principles of the Tenth Amendment would apply in this circumstance, so that directing state agencies to implement federal regulations would violate the "anti-commandeering" requirements of the Tenth Amendment. However, such a Tenth Amendment argument was rejected in *ACORN*. The court in that case noted that the Tenth Amendment has no application to Article I, § 4, which clearly contemplates that states will have the burden of administering federal elections. Thus, Article I, § 4, unlike most other provisions of the Constitution, is direct authority for Congress to regulate states as to the "Times, Places and Manner" of elections.[40]

The court in *ACORN* did note that there may be some theoretical limits to how Congress exercises its power under Article I, § 4. For instance, the court contemplated that if Congress attempted to use that power to "destroy state government" by deeming all employees of the state full-time federal voting registrars in order to make sure that every eligible federal voter in every state was registered, then the limits of the authority might be considered. However, the court found that requirements imposed by the Motor Voter Act or similar proposals did not represent an extraordinary financial or administrative burden on the state.

SPENDING POWER

Congress has expansive authority to spend money for the general welfare, which could encompass making monies available to state and local governments to modify their election procedures.[41] Further, the allocation of such grant monies could be conditioned on compliance by state or local officials with national standards for election procedures.[42] Such grant conditions need not be limited by the authority of Congress discussed above to directly legislate on the issue, but could address election procedures regardless of whether they were for the House, Senate, presidential, state, or local elections.[43]

End Notes

[1] P.L. 107-252.

[2] 42 U.S.C. § 15301(a)(1)-(5).

[3] 42 U.S.C. § 15301(a)(6).

[4] 42 U.S.C. § 15483(a)(4).

[5] U.S. Const. Art. I, §2, cl. 1 states "[t]he House of Representatives shall be composed of Members chosen every second Year by the People of the several States.... "

[6] Smiley v. Holm, 285 U.S. 355 (1932) (Congress may delegate authority to draw member districts to state legislatures, exclusive of governor's veto). For a history of Congressional regulation of federal elections, see Congressional Research Service, Constitution of the United States, Analysis and Interpretation 119 (1992) (available at http://www. loc.gov/crs/conan/art01/42.htm).

[7] 285 U.S. at 366. See Roudebush v. Hartke, 405 U.S. 15, 24-25 (1972) (state's authority to regulate recount of elections); United States v. Gradwell, 243 U.S. 476, 483 (1917) (full authority over federal election process, from registration to certification of results); United States v. Mosley, 238 U.S. 383, 386 (1915) (authority to enforce the right to cast ballot and have ballot counted); In re Coy, 127 U.S. 731, 752 (1888) (authority to regulate conduct at any election coinciding with federal contest); Ex parte Yarbrough, 110 U.S. 651, 662 (1884) (authority to make additional laws for free, pure, and safe exercise of right to vote); Ex parte Clarke, 100 U.S. 399, 404 (1879) (authority to punish state election officers for violation of state duties vis-a-vis Congressional elections). See also United States v. Simms, 508 F.Supp. 1179, 1183-85 (W.D. La.1979) (criminalizing payments in reference to registration or voting does not offend Tenth Amendment); Prigmore v. Renfro, 356 F.Supp. 427, 430 (N.D. Ala.1972) (absentee ballot program upheld as applied to federal elections), aff'd, 410 U.S. 919 (1973); Fowler v. Adams, 315 F.Supp. 592, 594 (M.D. Fla.1970), appeal dismissed, 400 U.S. 986 (1971) (authority to exact 5 percent filing fee for Congressional elections).

[8] U.S. Const. Art. II, §1, cl. 2 provides that "Each State shall appoint, in such Manner as the Legislature thereof may direct, a Number of Electors, equal to the whole Number of Senators and Representatives to which the State may be entitled in the Congress: but no Senator or Representative, or Person holding an Office of Trust or Profit under the United States, shall be appointed an Elector."

[9] 290 U.S. 534 (1934). See also Buckley v. Valeo, 424 U.S. 1, 67, 91 (1976)(upholding regulation of campaign financing by the Federal Election Campaign Act of 1971).

[10] 290 U.S. at 544-545.

[11] 290 U.S. 543-544.

[12] 42 U.S.C. §§1973gg et seq.

[13] ACORN v. Edgar, 56 F.3d 791 (7th Cir. 1995); Voting Rights Coalition v. Reno, 60 F.3d 1411, 1414 (9th Cir. 1995); ACORN v. Miller, 129 F.3d 833, 836 n.1 (1997).

[14] 56 F.3d at 793.

[15] Further support for this position is seen in Oregon v. Mitchell, where Justice Black wrote " ... it is the prerogative of Congress to oversee the conduct of presidential and vice-presidential elections and to set the qualifications for voters for electors for those offices. It cannot be seriously contended that Congress has less power over the conduct of presidential elections than it has over congressional elections." 400 U.S. 112, 124 (1970)(upholding federal statute lowering minimum age for voters). Although Justice Black wrote the opinion of the

Court, no other Justice joined this portion of his opinion, as the other Justices instead focused on Congress's power under the 14th Amendment.

[16] In fact, a careful reading of Burroughs reveals that the opinion is not even an interpretation of Article II, §1 at all (as presumed in the ACORN case and by Justice Black in Oregon v. Mitchell), but rather an interpretation (albeit uncited) of Article I, §8, cl. 18, the Necessary and Proper Clause. See quoted text accompanying note 6.

[17] U.S. Const., Amend. XIII (prohibiting slavery), Amend. XIV (due process and equal protection) and Amend. XV (voting rights).

[18] "The right of citizens ... to vote shall not be denied ... on account of sex."

[19] "The right of citizens ... to vote ... shall not be denied ... by reason of failure to pay any poll tax.... "

[20] "The right of citizens ... to vote shall not be denied ... on account of age."

[21] *See, e.g.*, Voting Rights Act of 1965, P.L. 89-110, 79 Stat. 437 (codified as amended at 42 U.S.C. §§ 1971, 1973- 1973bb-1 (1992)).

[22] 384 U.S. 641 (1966).

[23] 521 U.S. 507 (1997).

[24] 42 U.S.C. §2000bb et seq.

[25] 494 U.S. 872 (1990)(neutral generally applicable laws may be applied to religious practices even if the law is not supported by a compelling governmental interest).

[26] 121 S. Ct. 525 (2000).

[27] See University of Alabama v. Garret,148 L. Ed. 2d 866 (2000).

[28] 426 U.S. 833 (1976).

[29] In *National League of Cities v. Usery*, the Court conceded that the legislation under attack, which regulated the wages and hours of certain state and local governmental employees, was undoubtedly within the scope of the Commerce Clause, but it cautioned that there are attributes of sovereignty attaching to every state government which may not be impaired by Congress, not because Congress may lack an affirmative grant of legislative authority to reach the matter, but because the Constitution prohibits it from exercising the authority in that manner.

[30] 469 U.S. 528 (1985). Justice Blackmun's opinion for the Court in *Garcia* concluded that the *National League of Cities* test for "integral operations" in areas of traditional governmental functions had proven impractical, and that the Court in 1976 had "tried to repair what did not need repair."

[31] See also South Carolina v. Baker, 485 U.S. 505 (1988).

[32] 505 U.S. 144 (1992).

[33] 521 U.S. 898 (1997).

[34] 42 U.S.C. §§ 1973gg et seq.

[35] Smiley v. Holm, 285 U.S. 355, 366, (1932); *Ex parte* Siebold, 100 U.S. 371 (1879); United States v. Original Knights of the Ku Klux Klan, 250 F. Supp. 330, 351-55 (E.D. La. 1965) (three-judge court).

[36] ACORN v. Edgar, 56 F.3d 791 (7th Cir. 1995); Voting Rights Coalition v. Reno, 60 F.3d 1411, 1414 (9th Cir. 1995); ACORN v. Miller, 129 F.3d 833, 836 n.1 (1997).

[37] 56 F.3d 791 (7th Cir. 1995).

[38] United States v. Classic, 313 U.S. 299, 85 L. Ed. 1368, 61 S. Ct. 1031 (1941) ("Where the state law has made the primary an integral part of the procedure of choice, or where in fact the primary effectively controls the choice, the right of the elector to have his ballot counted at the primary is likewise included in the right protected by [law].")

[39] 56 F.3d at 794. U.S. Const., Art. I, § 8. "Let the end be legitimate; let it be within the scope of the Constitution, and all means which are appropriate, which are plainly adapted to that end, which are not prohibited, but consist with the letter and spirit of the Constitution, are constitutional." McCulloch v. Maryland, 17 U.S. (4 Wheat) 316 (1819).

[40] 56 F.3rd at 796.

[41] U.S. Const., Art. I, §8, cl. 1 provides that "The Congress shall have Power To lay and collect Taxes, Duties, Imposts and Excises, to pay the Debts and provide for the common Defence and general Welfare of the United States.... "

[42] South Dakota v. Dole, 483 U.S. 203 (1987)(Congress may condition grants to states based on criteria related to the underlying grant scheme).

[43] 483 U.S. at 208-09.

INDEX

D

E

F

G

H

I

J

L

M

N

O

P